dare
to
love
your
husband
well

T0105127

dare to love your husband well

A 90-DAY DEVOTIONAL FOR CHRIST-CENTERED WIVES

SARA DAIGLE

Good Books

New York, New York

Good Books books may be purchased in bulk at special discounts for sales promotion, corporate gifts, fund-raising, or educational purposes. Special editions can also be created to specifications. For details, contact the Special Sales Department, Good Books, 307 West 36th Street, 11th Floor, New York, NY 10018 or info@skyhorsepublishing.com.

Good Books is an imprint of Skyhorse Publishing, Inc.®, a Delaware corporation.

Visit our website at www.goodbooks.com.

10 9 8 7 6 5 4 3 2

Library of Congress Cataloging-in-Publication Data is available on file.

Cover design by Mona Lin
Cover photo image courtesy of istockphoto.com

Print ISBN: 978-1-68099-339-4
Ebook ISBN: 978-1-68099-340-0

Printed in China

Introduction

I stood in the old red barn with 400 others, worshiping my heart out on that chilly fall night. The crowd was large, and the rafters glowed with lights strung across the length of the barn. Since a multichurch worship gathering calls for someone to do security, my husband was outside while I stood near the front, staring up at open windows.

I was worshiping with many others, but it struck me that I was alone and responsible for my own experience. The worship of those around me was not enough to make my own heart worship—I had to choose to worship, choose to give God glory. And as I prayed over this book, I realized that we, as wives, have daily heart decisions to make, too.

No one can choose for you. No one will hold your hand at the end of life and say, "Honey, I'll be right next to you when you stand before God, and I'll explain why you were so angry. I'll tell God what kind of man your husband was and He'll understand why you became the kind of woman you are." God already understands, already knows. And He still wants your heart, now, fully. He still wants you to choose Him, every time, even amidst the heartache, the hurts, the misunderstandings in your marriage. And choosing God means daring to love your husband well.

The biblical principals you'll discover in these devotions have little to do with your husband. They have everything to do with you, because only you are responsible for your answer to your heavenly Father. When you follow His way, He leads you to wellness, not weakness—and you begin to see that freedom is available regardless of how your husband leads (or doesn't lead) your home!

You will also see that God means to cultivate your voice, not silence it. He wants to bring you to wholeness, not cause you to feel wholly lacking. Though He asks you to honor your man, He never asks you to be content without your own heart being honored, as well.

He wants you to give honor because that's who you are—an honorable woman who is loathe to disrespect herself or anyone around her, especially her man.

He wants to show you the beauty of cultivating personal goodness so you can share a life of goodness with your husband, rather than expect him to be your only life.

I've always thought that I'd rather love my husband well and do fewer other things, than do many great things while my husband remains lacking or unhappy in his relationship with me. That desire has led me on a journey of discovering his heart even as I discover my own. God has shown me that He, more than my husband, is my source of life. In letting go of my dependence on imperfect people, including my husband, I am able to hang on to a perfect God—and the result is an ever-increasing freedom that allows me to love better.

Through the scriptures explored in *Dare to Love Your Husband Well*, you will begin to formulate a biblical understanding of leadership and submission that allows you to thrive, because God never intended for leadership to deprive you of your gifts, silence your voice, or render you helpless in the face of abuse.

He's come to bring strength, joy, vitality, and a beautiful expression of all you are, so that, together with your man, you can celebrate all He is in both of you.

You are brave for embarking on this journey. Loving well requires honesty with yourself and your spouse, vulnerability, and trust that God wants what is best for you and your relationships. Ask God to move in your heart as you work through this book and to continue giving you the courage to pursue Him with all your heart. Because as you seek God, you may just find that your relationships begin to shift, too.

Day 1

"Likewise, husbands, live with your wives in an understanding way, showing honor to the woman as the weaker vessel, since they are heirs with you of the grace of life, so that your prayers may not be hindered." 1 Peter 3:7

Dare to embrace true thoughts on Godly womanhood while shedding false ideas you may have gleaned through life.

Honoring your husband well must spring from a bedrock of honoring yourself in the same way God does. He places high value on you, His daughter. You are a doorway, not a doormat. Though you serve, you are more than his servant. Though you meet his sexual needs, you are not a sex slave. Though you honor his leadership, you are not an employee or an oldest child. Though you defer to his leadership when the need arises, you remember that Godly leadership does not imply controlling lordship.

Honoring another never means throwing away your own honor. Loving your husband well means learning to honor him from a place of rest and joy, alive with purpose, and assured of your worth before a heavenly Father Who says you are a joint heir with your husband of the grace of life.

Placing yourself in a doormat position increases the emotional distance between you and your man (even if he does not know what causes the distance) and robs you both of romance and friendship. Living in the truth of who you are will free you up to honor your husband even more.

Father, help me know that I cannot experience the blessings of honoring another until I receive honor from You for my own self. I cannot give what I do not have. Assure me fully of Your heart toward me.

Today, dare believe that, though your roles are different, they are equal in importance. How are you going to strive for a lifestyle of mutual honor and respect with your man?

_____

_____

_____

_____

_____

_____

_____

_____

_____

_____

_____

_____

_____

_____

Day 2

"As Sarah obeyed Abraham, calling him lord. And you are her children, if you do good and do not fear anything that is frightening." 1 Peter 3:6

Sarah is held as an example of Godly submission to many young wives, yet her example is often misinterpreted to women who truly desire to do well by their men.

Sarah called Abraham lord, but she was strong enough to have opinions, as well. When the angels told Abraham that he and Sarah were going to have a son in their old age, she laughed and said, "After I am waxed old shall I have pleasure, my lord being old also?" (Genesis 18:12).

I want us to see this—Sarah's sin was not that she had an opinion, but that *her opinion discredited the faithfulness of God.*

A strong woman knows how to have opinions and host a mind of noble, worthy thought. Any teaching that says women should be without a voice is entirely flawed and has brought much damage to marriages.

A truly strong woman is a submissive woman who knows how to share her heart in love and respect. She knows how to give God credit by trusting Him with things beyond her ability or control. She knows how to be amazed, and live in wonder of His power.

She knows this so well that she does not hesitate to show honor to her man as she submits to his leadership. Through this heart posture, she honors the Lord by trusting Him to care for her, sometimes in spite of her man.

Father, show me clearly the value of my own heart
so that I can honor my man, as well.

Today, dare to have your opinion—then, take an even greater dare to honor God and your husband while expressing it! In what ways will you express yourself with honor today?

Day 3

"Love believes all things." 1 Corinthians 13:7

So, we're in bed laughing about it, now. Because years have taught us that fighting is so draining you may as well chuck the idea.

Fighting so that you can have more "love" isn't love at all. I've learned to stay up late with my man periodically, and he's learned to crawl into that bed with me long before he's ready—and then, stealthily creep back out of bed to live up his night-owl side.

Most of all, we've learned to let go of expectations. It's OK if he's a night owl and I'm a morning person who is so delighted with a fresh day I want to pull him right out of bed so we can plan all the wonderful things we could do. *I've learned not to beg him out of bed, but to get myself on that floor if that's what I want to do.*

He smiles at my giddiness in the morning and wishes I could be so thrilled about staying up late for a show.

I smile at his face, sleeping soundly in the morning hours, and wish he could be so thrilled about a schedule that allows for a quiet house at night and an early start to the day.

But see this—*we are smiling.* And we are coming together, *not because life makes everything perfect, but because perfect love makes a life.*

We will never be—and never have to be—that perfect couple who gets up early for coffee together before work. But we will always be that couple who kisses good-bye no matter what time of day or night it is.

None of this would happen if we hadn't learned to surrender expectations and let them go. Each day, we come together or we drift apart, and *the choice is ours more than changing each other is our choice.*

Life-changing love can't happen when you're so busy trying to change a life to fit your own that soon you don't fit together at all. Because being the same was never a prerequisite for true love; having mutual acceptance of each other is the key ingredient.

*God, help us to surrender expectations
and learn to love hard, instead.*

Today, dare to surrender your expectations of who your spouse "should" be and sink into love for each other instead. How will you show acceptance toward your husband today?

Day 4

"You prepare a table before me in the presence of my enemies." Psalm 23:5

What if you were to look deep into the heart for the cause of your pain, rather than running from the symptoms?

Searching for the root causes takes bravery—more strength than most couples can muster. This is why symptoms continue until the marriage is nearly in ruins. There's a new way, friends. Let's find it and utilize it! For more on this, I highly recommend reading *Love & Respect* by Dr. Emerson Eggerich (Thomas Nelson, 2004).

Finding the cause does not imply that you tolerate the symptoms—it merely gives you an even greater chance of ridding your marriage of them. If you dig up the root, the plant won't sprint up again year after year.

A dear friend spent time away from her husband because of a deep sin in his life that was destroying her emotionally. She spent this time searching deep into her own heart, and that of her husband's. While she honestly didn't know if she could ever live with him again, she kept working on root causes.

Today, her marriage is healed. They came together on an entirely different foundation. Because she was willing to look at the cause more than the symptoms (even though she left for a time because of nasty symptoms), her chance of renewal was much greater.

Today, decide not to take your man's actions personally, but realize that many aspects of his life have brought him to his present state. This way is redemptive; the other, human and natural. One way entirely opposed to human rights and reason; the other, full of supernatural love and care. Which does Christ show us?

Father, thank you that You understand our deepest hearts. You know what makes us want to react the way we do. Wash away the lingering roots in our lives so we can live healthily with each other.

Today, dare to find out what is causing your disconnect, whether it be him or you. How will you refuse to walk in apathy, discovering the root causes of your needs?

_____
_____
_____
_____
_____
_____
_____
_____
_____
_____
_____
_____
_____

Day 5

"Love hopes all things." 1 Corinthians 13:7

One couple was nearly destroyed by the wife's violent anger before they stepped into a counselor's office. She would become irate, defensive, and so out of control that her husband would be scared of her.

When she was asked to choose a small toy animal that best described her feelings during those times, she chose an angry bull with his head lowered in defense for battle.

The counselor asked the right questions, and before long she mentioned her mother putting her into her room as a young girl, then allowing men to use her for pay, which they handed to her mother on their way out the door. When she bit one man so hard that he left, she was no longer forced to comply, and her mother sent the men to her sister's room.

Her fierce reactions to unpleasant things in her marriage stemmed back to things her husband had no way to understand. He didn't know what to ask. He didn't know how to handle her, or help her. All he knew was that he needed to protect himself, and perhaps leave in the end.

Had he done so, he would have left her even more wounded and ready to fight. He would have destroyed their marriage and complicated the life of his kids.

But he really didn't know. And often, we really don't know. We remain entirely naive to the source of the problems in our spouse (or in ourselves) and thus end up making them even worse.

How many of us are reacting to our men rather than finding the heart in our men?

Next time your man offends you, how about asking him what he's experiencing and what he needs? Listen to him carefully, then repeat back what you've heard to make sure you're understanding him. Then, ask him what you can do to help.

Listening well means we listen to understand—not listen to formulate a swift rebuttal. Listening well implies drawing out, pondering his thoughts, and acknowledging them, whether or not you think they are right. Listening well must be part of loving your man well.

Lord, give me wisdom to know how to draw
out the heart of my man.

Dare to find out what drives your man. Listen to what he does even more than to what he says. How will you purpose to listen to his heart and life today?

_____

_____

_____

_____

_____

_____

_____

_____

Day 6

"Let each of you look not only to his own interests, but also to the interests of others." Philippians 2:4

"Your schedule affects me a lot," I tell my husband. "I do so many things without you."

"I feel like you're pressuring me without understanding that my body functions best on a late schedule," he replies.

I pause. Is he right? I feel lacking, and he feels less than cared for when I don't seem to get it that his body *really does work best* on a night schedule. How to merge? There seems to be an impasse right before us.

"I don't think I need us to be on the same bed and meal schedules as much as I need us to find ways to connect at other times," I tell him. "I feel lonely."

He wraps me in his arms and says, "I don't want you to feel lonely. We need to find answers for that."

Sometimes we need to agree on how to make our differences work more than we need to try so hard not to have differences. We need to identify the feeling we have more than change the circumstance or person that seems to cause the feeling in the first place.

We don't always need to reconstruct each other in order to come up with a constructive solution.

I can accept that my husband likes to work on a different schedule, while coming up with solutions for our schedules to meet at some point in the day. I can allow him to be his late night owl while I'm an early morning bird, as long as we fly on the same gust of wind.

Love him well by finding constructive solutions to your problems without always trying to reconstruct *him*!

Father, help me be attentive to my husband's needs even as I express my own. Help me to merge both our lives together rather than demanding that he change who You made him to be.

Today, dare to express your need in a way that also allows him to have needs and desires. How will you find a solution that will help both of you?

Day 7

"Help these women, who have labored side by side with
me in the gospel together with Clement and the rest of
my fellow workers, whose names are in the book of life."
Philippians 4:3

"Women shouldn't study theology," I hear. "They
should trust their husbands to seek truth, and all they need
to do is follow."

I'm saddened when I hear those words from a Christ-fol-
lower. Have we forgotten that the Greek word for *help-meet*
is *ezer,* the same word that is mostly used for God, and always used to describe help in vitally important situations?

Christian woman, you are not behind your man, or left
in the dust by your man. You are seated beside him as a
warrior princess, benefiting from spiritual blessings just as
your man does.

The word *ezer* is often used in terms of rescue; do you
believe that your man may need you to rescue him by
bringing life he doesn't see?

Ezer is used twice in reference to Eve; thrice for helping
(or not helping) in life-threatening circumstances, and six-
teen times for God. Why then is the term *help-meet* used to
make wives feel "out of place" when they study, reason,
and ponder things of importance?

When we subject ourselves blindly to any human being
by blinding ourselves to the Word of God, we are guilty
of not honoring the Word. And hear this—if a man is offended when you speak, live, and act in the Spirit, he is
defending his own kingdom while his heart is dulled to the
realities of God. When you are in tune with God, you can
speak truth in the presence of a Godly man, and he will
receive it because his spirit is also in tune with God.

Rather than barbed wire entering the atmosphere when you speak, there will be a mutual acceptance of God's truth. Get into your Bibles; God needs us to have vision just as much as our men, and if we don't, we are both more susceptible to ruin. You are his *ezer*—and an *ezer* does a whole lot more than caring for the physical needs of one's husband. In grasping this truth, never let go of caring for him, but also never stifle the mind and spirit God has gifted you with.

Lord, forgive us for reducing Christian women to people with less capability of absorbing Your truth. Help us rise up and help change the spiritual atmosphere in which we live.

Dare to believe you were created with the same spiritual blessings available to you as are available to your husband. How will you make good use of this privilege?

_____

_____

_____

_____

_____

_____

Day 8

"And He sat down and called the twelve. And he said to them, 'If anyone would be first, he must be last of all and servant of all.'" Mark 9:35

I squeeze the rag empty and hand it to two little kids, then show them how to scrub away. They make a game out of cleaning, and I snap some pictures of their cute faces. Those years when they were all very small were a great joy even though I stayed home with them all day long.

Service is beautiful. Our culture tells us otherwise—but happy is the wife who takes joy in handing her man a cup of coffee, cleaning the home, and cooking up meals.

Mundane chores can turn into meaningful ways of expressing love when we see the beauty of it. Being a strong woman has nothing to do with proving our competence outside of the home, but everything to do with how we give wherever we are. Though some women have other jobs, careers, and callings, we get it all wrong when we think we need one to prove our competence.

When we see the beauty of turning a house into a peaceful home, we do not loathe common chores or think it less than dignified to work at home. When the home is well cared for, children thrive, and your man finds a place of solace and rest from his working world.

Give willingly, gladly, and grace your man's world with the nurture God has designed you to give. Run an errand for him, make sure his laundry is taken care of, and keep his favorite creamer in the fridge. Each small act of service culminates in a happy marriage with effects that reach far outside your walls.

Lord, forgive me for disregarding service, when Your example shows that You came to serve. Help me create a place of rest and peace for my husband.

Today's dare is to embrace service, knowing that service speaks volumes of love to your man and creates a peaceful haven for him to rejuvenate. How will you serve him today?

Day 9

"You have turned for me my mourning into dancing;
You have loosed my sackcloth, and clothed me with
gladness." Psalm 30:11

She's a crazy woman, but she's a happy woman.

And her man, well, he's crazy, too. But he's happy. They don't seem to need the typical American family life to be happy, either.

He had dreams, and she, good woman that she is, didn't want her man to fall into that typical midlife crisis, so she jumped on board and began soaring with the wind. Life didn't consist of the perfect Saturday walking through town, latte in hand, double stroller pushed by her man. (You know, the things those *perfect* couples do that make us all a little wistful?)

Life was crazy wild. Saturdays looked more like her alone with the kids while he pursued his dreams, and then all of them enjoying a cozy but late dinner together when he finally made it home.

But let's get this—this couple is happier than most any couple I know. *Because you don't need the "perfect" life in order to have, maintain, and grow perfect love.*

Working toward a perfect life when you're not filled with perfect love will render you stale and lifeless. Why do we women have an idea that joy is found in things and circumstances more than in matters of the heart?

You could have your perfect date night but be unhappy while you're sitting in that booth, beautifully done up in your black dress. But if you focus on the heart of your relationship rather than the things in your relationship, you will find happiness and joy *everywhere*.

God, help me learn to soar with the wind and lean right into joy.

Today, dare to release expectations and grab hold of love instead! How will you accept love even when it's given in ways you're not looking for?

_____
_____
_____
_____
_____
_____
_____
_____
_____
_____
_____
_____
_____
_____
_____

Day 10

"The Lord is the strength of His people; He is the saving refuge of His anointed." Psalm 28:8

I just wrote a text to my husband yesterday, asking if he would support me in taking a month to write. He said *yes.*

He said yes, knowing that I probably wouldn't cook dinners as often as I normally do, that I would be unable to join him at the gym, and that life for everyone would be altered, and more difficult.

This means a lot to me, because of all people, his opinion and support means most. On the flip side, my opinion and support of his work means most to him.

I didn't expect him to be a law enforcement officer—and I dare say he didn't expect having a wife typing madly for a month on some book deadline. Neither of us knew what life would turn us into. But we say *yes* to each other.

Are you saying yes to your man?

Because of the job my husband loves, my life consists of constantly varied schedules and heading to bed alone most nights. We have few meals together. Sometimes, he works on Christmas day—and often, he's rushing out the door on nights when other women have their guys by their side.

My love language is quality time, so this one is huge. But ladies, when it comes down to it, wouldn't we rather see our men happy and fulfilled, with less time, than have all the time in the world while he remains unfulfilled? When they're happy in their vocation, they are happier in their home. In the long run, it's a win-win.

Get behind him and learn to grow with the ride. *Doing life well often means letting go of what we thought life would look like.* When we let go, we find ourselves surprised with joy—and we learn to really live by catching delight in all of it.

Father, thank You that wellness comes from You.
Help me live my life from a place of wholeness in
Someone greater than my husband so that we can support
each other in what You've called us to

Today, dare to remind yourself that your support of him means as much as his support and love of you. How will you show your support of him today?

_____

_____

_____

_____

_____

_____

_____

_____

_____

_____

_____

Day 11

"Come with me from Lebanon, my bride . . . you have captivated my heart." Song of Solomon 4:8a & 9a

He comes into my house, calling my name—and every time, I run into his arms, laughing. Have you ever heard of such fun? I love being his "always buddy."

I went a little wild with delight when I heard this comment. His "always buddy." Ah!

This couple has been married for forty-seven years. She's learned to accompany her man, or not accompany him, but to always be there when he calls her name. Her heart is there with him, for him—and she's *into him.*

Your man needs a friend. Deep in the heart of every man is the craving for companionship; it just may look different to him than it does to you.

My man likes me to take time. I'm busy rushing about doing a hundred things, and he loves when I pause, perhaps to join him on the floor while he does his routine of stretching. Perhaps I'll stop for a moment alone with him in the kitchen when I could (and think I should) finish the next chore. Sometimes, we won't have an actual date for months, but our friendship grows if we're still finding moments to connect throughout the week, and caring for each other's heart.

Men have hearts that need many of the same things our hearts crave, though we might express it differently. Let's find out what speaks love to our man, and cultivate friendship by actively pursuing their language. Is it time together? Loving words? Physical contact? Maybe he feels loved when you send him an affirming text, or maybe it's when you rub his shoulders or slip your hand into his.

Let's be specific and intentional about speaking our spouse's language—and don't be afraid to tell your husband what makes *you* feel loved. Learning to speak a other than the one than we naturally speak is well worth the effort!

Lord, help us be true friends, cultivating affection, realizing that all friendships need certain ingredients to thrive.

Today, dare to do something specific that makes your husband feel loved. If you're not sure what, ask him! And notice when he does something that makes you feel especially loved, and thank him for it!

_____

_____

_____

_____

_____

_____

_____

_____

_____

Day 12

"Do not lie to one another, seeing that you have put off the old self with its practices." Colossians 3:9

I used to shift around, hint around, and *expect around*. But when I heard my husband express that he just likes to be told what I need or want, I realized I'd been wasting a lot of time.

Ladies, we have this thing of hiding our true feelings *all wrong*. Do you realize how frustrating it is for a man to see his beloved upset about something he did or didn't do when she never told him what she wanted from him?

If we can get one thing into our heads, it should be this: *your man probably will not read your mind and automatically know what you want him to know.*

This one still makes me cringe. How can I ask him for time together? Why doesn't he just know I need it, and I needed it a month ago, and now it's been two months and I'm *really* needing it? Should I really need to ask him?

So we remain silent, and the festering begins. Expectations quickly turn into premeditated resentment, and before long two people who fell in love wonder how they fell out of love.

Asking for what you want is not as hard as you think it is. It can be as simple as, "Hey Hon, I'd love to play tennis with you this weekend! Want to?" Or even, "I'm really missing you. Could we spend some time together soon?"

Your man will be relieved to leave out the guesswork. He can decline if it doesn't work for him, or he can plan something with you—but what matters most is that you were honest with your need, and able to express that need to him. You were fair and gave him a chance before living with resentment or complaining to your girlfriends about how lonely you are.

Allow your man to rise to the occasion by asking him if there could be an occasion, however small it may be!

Lord, help me not to judge my man before giving him a chance to hear me. Help me treat him in fairness and love.

Today, dare to tell your man what you need, clearly! Then, take it a step further and dare stay in the love-path even if things don't work out as you hoped. How will you meet each other's needs while still respecting your differences?

_____

_____

_____

_____

_____

_____

_____

_____

_____

_____

_____

Day 13

"Do your best to present yourself to God as one approved, a worker who has no need to be ashamed, rightly handling the word of truth." 2 Timothy 2:15

My man used to be a carpenter, and I've admired his precisely done, beautiful work many times.

But the other day, as he rushed to paint a leaking upper-deck floor, he splashed specks of white paint all over the brown walls.

I was bewildered and stared in disbelief—then, I mentioned it.

"I figured this deck wasn't used much, and it's ugly already," he said. "And I'm in a rush."

I stood there silently. I loved my deck and disagreed that it was ugly. The messy paint job was going to drive me crazy. But something kept me from speaking up right away. A day later I thanked him for fixing the leak, fixing my closet shelves, and for buying this great home for us to enjoy.

I did it on purpose. And I avoided mentioning the deck on purpose. The time will come when I ask him if he'd mind fixing it, or maybe I'll run upstairs with a paint brush and do it myself. But snapping at him in that moment of frustration, when he was in a hurry and trying to do something helpful, wouldn't have helped either of us. Some things are serious enough to merit immediate dialogue, even in the heat of the moment. Splattered paint on a wall is not one of those things.

Much of the time, what matters is how we speak and when we speak. There's no need to demean your man. Don't make him feel like a little boy who hasn't done a good job for his mama. When we act like his mama, we throw water on his fire rather than fuel to keep it burning.

But men do want and need honesty. I could leave the deck alone, but truth is, I need to speak or act because this really bothers me. I won't do it until the time is right—and then, I won't accuse, belittle, or demand. I will express, ask, and share my heart. Let's love our man well by sharing our thoughts well!

Father, grant me Your timing and grace. Help me to know when to speak up immediately and when to wait or let things go.

Today, dare to request rather than require, to wait for him rather than wilt him, to ask instead of accuse. In what ways can you improve your communication with your man today?

_____

_____

_____

_____

_____

_____

_____

_____

Day 14

"Out of them shall come songs of thanksgiving, and the voices of those who celebrate." Jeremiah 30:19a

Our son had just turned six years old. He had asked for a small party, so when the few gifts were opened, he turned to me and asked, "Where are my other gifts?"

"You only wanted a few people here, son, so all your gifts have been opened," I explained. Feeling badly that he expressed his disappointment in front of our generous guests, I continued, "What else were you hoping for?"

"A blanket," he replied.

That's when his little blond-haired friend waltzed into the room with a delighted grin on her face and handed him her very own blanket wrapped around an ancient toy truck. Never mind that the blanket was stained and the truck was broken. She handed it to David with a confident look that said, *I just solved all your problems.*

David stared. "This blanket is dirty!" he declared loudly. "And this truck is broken."

"That's why I gave it to you!" Mari announced.

The adults sat in helpless gales of laughter while I harbored secret embarrassment and distress. My son defied everything I had tried to teach him—that parties are not all about gifts, and that gratefulness trumps the accumulation of material things. He never once understood or appreciated her simple desire to satisfy his wishes for a blanket, and her willingness to give him her own.

How many times do our men try to love on us while we turn a dissatisfied face the other way and continue in discontentment? Instead of expecting to be loved a certain way, what if we learned to receive the love they are already showing us?

One wife struggled for years with the lack of heart-to-heart sharing in her marriage, while others noticed the extravagant love glowing from his eyes whenever he looked at her and longed for the same. He didn't know how to communicate as well as some people, but ladies, *he adored her.*

If your man adores you, if he tries his best to love on you, allow yourself to notice and appreciate it. Not every woman has a man who cares for her. We may gripe about our lack in certain areas while entirely missing out on the love being extended our way.

Today, let's ask ourselves, "Am I loved?" If the answer is yes, let's lean into it, appreciate it, soak it up, and grow the love we have. From that platform of appreciation, we can then make requests for the other things we desire. But if those things aren't easy for him to give, let's be patient and keep right on receiving the love he already shows!

Father, help me to know how much I'm loved by You and by my husband. Help me to soak it in rather than resist it when it's not given in the way I want.

Today, take a dare to watch for love. Then, receive it wholeheartedly and allow the warmth of it to soften the hard places of your heart. What can you find to rejoice in today?

Day 15

"Christ is faithful over God's house as a son. And we are His house if indeed we hold fast our confidence and our boasting in our hope." Hebrews 3:6

Seeking to perfect our inner peace by perfecting our surroundings is shifting sand and only calls for another foundation to be laid for our peace. One day, my man and I had one of those hard conversations, the kind where you just can't seem to get on the same page. What we needed from each other didn't come naturally to either of us.

Instead of listening to each other, we tried to fix each other. It didn't work; it never does.

And then it sunk in. What if I really listened in on his heart? What if I allowed him to be his own man rather than trying to fix him into my version of a "perfect" man?

While many women bring up conflict in order to connect, a man often sees it as another attempt to control. Women may have the best of intentions while a man reads the worst into them. To grow each other, we are under a divine mandate to do what does not come naturally. This means tapping in to supernatural wisdom and grace.

What if, rather than justify ourselves, we tried just as hard to give an ear to the other? What if we listened to what each other was *doing* as much as we listened to what they were *saying*?

Next time you're in a messy conversation, step back and pause your rapid thoughts. Dare to shut your mouth and listen, really listen, to your man.

Human nature pulls from others; God's nature pours onto others. Growth happens best when love is poured rather than when the rope is pulled.

Father, help me to listen well, and allow my man a place of peace and an environment of growth.

Only the brave dare take their boat onto unchartered waters. Dare to believe that the very thing that may cause you to feel weak is, in fact, the very thing that proves your strength. How will you show your husband that you hear him and understand him today?

_____

_____

_____

_____

_____

_____

_____

_____

_____

_____

_____

_____

_____

_____

Day 16

"And He said, 'My presence will go with you, and I will give you rest.'" Exodus 33:14

I can't help but hear the guys at the gun shop as one says to the other, "Don't tell your wife about this," to which the other replies, "Oh, I won't tell her about this at all. She would be so upset." The first man agrees, "Yeah, she's always upset about something."

Hiding things is at the top of the list of things I hate—but here, I saw a man who was obviously living with much control and condemnation, making it difficult to be honest with his wife.

An honoring woman is able to let go of things. She knows God's heart is for her to honor her husband whether or not he makes the decisions she thinks he should. Remember that honor does not imply believing he's right. Honor is a heart posture you extend to everyone, even when you disagree.

When you surround your man with condemnation, you make it harder for his heart to accept God's conviction.

Express your heart clearly, not in hints. Be very honest; then release it. Clear communication allows you to hand things over to the Lord, knowing you've already done your part.

After expressing your heart, make sure you don't permeate the atmosphere with condemnation and disapproval. This doesn't mean you can't have your own emotions as you process. It does mean that you won't allow bitterness to permeate your home.

Love your husband well by sharing your thoughts with him, but releasing him to live his life.

Father, give me grace to communicate clearly, but at the same time, clear the way of condemnation.

Dare to allow the Holy Spirit be the One to bring conviction to your husband. Dare to speak, then, take an even greater dare to let go and stop nagging. How will you release him, today?

_____

_____

_____

_____

_____

_____

_____

_____

_____

_____

_____

_____

_____

_____

Day 17

"My beloved speaks and says to me, 'Arise, my love, my beautiful one, and come away, for behold, the winter is past; the rain is over and gone. The flowers appear on the earth, the time of singing has come.'" The Song of Solomon 2:10-12a

I'm sitting at Starbucks this morning, typing away—but I'm doing something else, too; I'm observing people. And I'm brave enough to ask an elderly gentleman if he'd be part of my survey.

"What do you need most from your wife?" I ask.

He pauses and smiles, "Friendship, companionship, and honesty. When she goes to Seattle to see our kids, I miss her."

He's elderly, and smiling. And I picture his wife, who must also be elderly, and no longer spry and nimble. Fifty-seven years is a long time. I'm awed by this love lasting longer than I've existed, and I see it again. Honesty and friendship go a long way in the heart of a man. Women may joke about a man needing sex, respect, and food—but truth is, they need love and companionship, as well.

Women, it's time to let go of resentment and give way to release. Maybe you need to start from scratch and rebuild your friendship from the ground up, or maybe you need to dig through your past to figure out where the resentment came from so you can deal with the cause and lessen the effects of it wisely. Find a counselor; ask for help.

Whatever you do, refuse to live with a cold heart. Be honest with the fact that you need answers. Then set about learning how to be your man's friend—he probably craves it as much as you do!

Father, help me to let go of resentment and give way to release.
Help me know why I'm not warm toward my husband, and
what to do about it.

Today, dare believe that the things you long for are yours to have. Dare believe that God has created you a free agent, which means you get to choose freedom and love—even if your man does not. In what areas will you allow God to release you?

Day 18

"For the word of God is living and active, sharper than any two-edged sword, piercing to the division of soul and of spirit, of joints and of marrow, and discerning the thoughts and intentions of the heart." Hebrews 4:12

My husband sat there waiting, wondering why I wouldn't answer. Meanwhile, I was desperately trying to decide which response would make him happiest or cause less conflict. And get this—both of us hated it. When I finally let go of needing his approval on all fronts, we were both much happier.

Respecting your man does not always mean pleasing him; it simply means that you do not attack, belittle, or wound him. When you have a problem, you address the problem without attacking *him.*

Much of it depends not on whether you talk, but on how you talk. Honesty without anger or spite is a beautiful avenue for closeness. Pretense always separates and leads to a superficial, artificial relationship that will leave both of you longing for true intimacy. False peace breeds loneliness.

When you are loving, grateful, and kind, you open the doorway for honesty about difficult subjects. Drench your spouse in so much love and appreciation that you can also be honest about the things that bother you.

Communicating honestly must be done from a bedrock of appreciation and approval. If there's no foundation, honesty will hurt and wound your spouse. Feed your spouse's heart more than you drain it. Be honest with all the difficult things, but sustain his heart with appreciation and thankfulness so there is a healthy foundation to speak from.

Father, help me show appreciation to my husband so much that when I come to him with grievances, there will be a foundation of love to speak from.

Today, dare to build a foundation of thankfulness. Build it strong, build it well. How will you show appreciation for your man today?

Day 19

"Rather, speaking the truth in love, we are to grow up
in every way into him who is the head, into Christ . . ."
Ephesians 4:15, ESV

"My husband didn't want to come to church for a
while," she said, "and I didn't want to badger him. But I
wanted to go, myself. So I went, and I didn't badger him to
come with me. Last Sunday, he came to church for my sake
and he said he enjoyed it!"

"It's so important to have a voice," she continued. "I try
to listen well and not make him feel like he has to be me,
feel what I feel, or do what I do. I allow him to be his own
person because I know we are different."

This woman knows honor on a high level. She gives it
as she retains her own. Do you see how she honors him
by freeing him but also expresses her desires and is able to
release him while pursuing them?

She didn't just go to church—she was actively involved
in ministry. Often, he would come to support her, and we
both knew he probably would not have come willingly had
she badgered him into a guilty attendance. She did what
she needed to do and let him do what he was doing.

"We are a team," she says. "A team that he leads." She
counts herself a worthy part of their team, and her desires
are never hidden in a false pretense of "submission." She's
honest, and in honoring her man she doesn't lose her own
honor. She defers to him without denying her own heart
needs. She allows him to lead without losing her voice.

She and her man are one of the happiest couples I know.
Let's learn from her and free our man not to feel what we
feel, think what we think, or even believe what we believe.
Let's join her honesty, but also join her letting go.

Lord, help me free my husband from needing to be me in order to have my love. Help me pursue my desires without forcing my husband to join me.

Today's dare is to cast off pressure, condemnation, or nagging—and to put on freedom, speak the truth in love, and walk in joy. How will you release your husband today while pursuing your own needs?

Day 20

"When justice is done, it is a joy to the righteous."
Proverbs 21:15

She asked me over the phone, "Should I agree to have sex with my husband even if he can't let go of this other girl?"

I told her, *no*. A true understanding of honor includes respecting yourself enough to stand up when the need arises. Godly women are not called to be doormats. Sometimes, a wife is called to stand up and allow the pieces to fly *if they will*. You were never meant to be responsible for your man's heart; you were meant to respond to God's heart.

I've seen countless women suffer in silence while the men in their lives misuse or mistreat them. In time, if she does not stand up and get the help she needs, she will wilt and become lifeless.

When we focus so much on submission but not on other aspects of Godliness for women, we end up with bowed shoulders and dull apathy because we wrongly live as though we have no kingdom rights. This is false, dangerous, and will steal the breath out of your lungs. A wife who does not see her own value to the Lord will resent the very honor she tries to show.

You cannot truly honor another unless you respect yourself. *Showing honor becomes a wellspring of life when it is shown by a heart who knows honor personally.* Just as people who are hurting are more likely to hurt others, so those who respect themselves are more likely to respect others.

When we fully take our place as women of honor, we value ourselves as the Lord does. That's a high value! From that premise of joy and delight in our place with the Father, we begin to understand respect and honor. We respect

God enough to realize His heart toward us—and it is never to take advantage of us.

Showing honor flows as a result of realizing who we already are—loved, destined for purpose, called to be princess warriors with strength of character and vision.

Lord, help those who suffer in silence to reach out, speak out, and begin to walk out of bondage. Help us see the life we are called to live.

Today, if you are mistreated and disrespected, dare speak up and ask for more. Dare to stand as one who is also worthy of love and respect. How will you ask your man, in an honoring manner, for right treatment if he's mistreating you?

Day 21

"Wives, submit to your own husbands, as to the Lord.
For the husband is the head of the wife even as Christ is
the head of the church, his body, and is himself its Savior.
Now as the church submits to Christ, so also wives
should submit in everything to their husbands. Husbands,
love your wives, as Christ loved the church and gave
himself up for her, that he might sanctify her, having
cleansed her by the washing of water with the word . . ."
Ephesians 5:22–26

"Do you have a voice in your marriage?" I ask, because
I know her man's happy—and so is she.

"Oh, yes," she assures me. "I'm very honest and I never
pretend. We talk about everything before we make a deci-
sion. But in the end, if we still differ, I allow him to lead.
If he still wants one thing when I want another, I don't
insist on my own way. He often defers to me, but when he
doesn't, I let it go."

Her words didn't surprise me because I could tell she
had a voice—and I could tell he was honored. She continued, "When I really need something, heaven and earth
move for it to happen. I was the one who said we should
move to Washington; I was the one who picked out our
home. My man really honors my voice."

All this from the same lady who said that her man is
leader and she defers to him? How does *that* line up? She
says to the rest of us, "When we allow our men to lead,
they often do everything they can to accommodate our desires when we feel strongly about something."

Though this is true, we do not honor our man just so
he honors us. This turns him into a project rather than a
recipient of the grace of God in our lives. Rather, we show

honor because God asks us to do so, and we follow God regardless of the outcome. Being in tune with God, more than getting our needs met, is our goal.

Trust that God will provide for your needs even when your husband may not. When we forget this truth, we begin to live, think, and act in ways we think will fill our needs rather than in ways we know God is leading us.

Lord, help me honor my husband's lead in our home while sharing my heart and thoughts with him.

Today's dare is to be very honest, but very honoring. It is to defer to his leadership while maintaining your place on the team. How will you defer to him when the need rises?

_____
_____
_____
_____
_____
_____
_____
_____
_____

Day 22

"Blessed are the peacemakers, for they shall be called
[daughters] of God." Matthew 5:9

What about honoring a man who doesn't deserve honor?

Men know it takes supernatural power to honor another when he doesn't deserve it. I'm sure your husbands find it difficult to show respect to a demanding boss or a crooked political figure. This very difficulty in his own life is what will astound him if he sees it lived well by you.

The grace in you will be seen as supernatural—and therefore, a means to draw him to Christ. He will know you possess strength not usually shown by human hearts—and he will admire it, however loathe he is to show it.

Ladies of unsaved men, take great courage! Your life of love and honor to your husband may well be the strongest voice God will ever bring to his heart. *In a sense you are a missionary, an ambassador.* This is a great honor.

Seeing your own worth and calling in the Lord's eyes will give you the strength you need to bear with an unsaved or selfish man.

No matter what you do, he may not change. Women are not responsible for their husband's actions or his walk with the Lord, but only their own. In all of this, God has wired a man to be fascinated with his wife—and he will be quite taken with your ability to show honor when he knows he doesn't deserve it.

Father, thank You that I am a free agent and can choose to walk in the good and best even when my husband does not.

If you are married to an unsaved man, make your dare a big, brave one. Dare to walk as a saved woman even though you live with an unsaved man. How will you show him your salvation?

Day 23

"I have learned in whatever situation I am to be content. I know how to be brought low, and I know how to abound." Philippians 4:11&12a

"Is she prettier than me?"
"Will she like me?"
"Will I look bad if I hang out with a girl that beautiful?"

Many of us try to find our identity in a visible place while forgetting that it was formed in the womb by God when we were yet entirely invisible to others.

When the God of the universe declares our identity and forms us as He wants us, we stoop low when we compare ourselves with others. We lose our dignity. We place ourselves, though involuntarily, in a humanistic realm where our worth is based on what we cannot control.

Jesus, though God, didn't consider equality with God a thing to strive for. What did He hold as the most important thing? Doing His Father's will.

It's not about us, sisters. That insecure thought leads you to believe that you are more important than God. When God is the One we are concerned with, we agree with God in His creation of us. This frees us to live confidently in all areas of life, including enjoying sexual intimacy even when we dislike certain areas of our bodies.

Loving your husband well means that you must first accept well who God created you to be. Your man needs you to be confident more than perfect, to utilize your gifts more than compare your gifts, to cultivate your beauty rather than grasp for the beauty you think you don't have.

Father, help me live confidently and wholly so that I am able to love my husband from a place of peace.

Today, dare chuck this world and its standards of success or worth. Then, claim your identity and purpose here on this Earth. In what ways will you embrace truth today?

_____

_____

_____

_____

_____

_____

_____

_____

_____

_____

_____

_____

_____

_____

_____

_____

Day 24

"Bearing with one another and, if one has a complaint against another, forgiving each other; as the Lord has forgiven you, so you also must forgive." Colossians 3:13

I hate conflict—as in, hate it so much that something inside curls up tightly in a ball of tension and every nerve in me wants to spin out of control as I try to stay focused. I'm not sure why, except that I was raised with little conflict around me and have always associated it with the purely negative.

I'm slowly learning to expect conflict and be OK when it happens. I'm learning that most close friends experience conflict, and truth be told, the closer my friends have been, the more opportunity there has been for difficulty. Most of the time, I'm able to work through those things and move on with a deeper understanding of my friends and what they need.

Rather than viewing conflict with our spouses as a threat to intimacy, we can view it as a tool for greater intimacy. Embracing conflict is better than the alternative fake harmony that happens when we hide away out of fear. People who run from conflict are usually afflicted with all sorts of unresolved problems—because life brings problems no matter how hard we try to deny them access. The brave in heart accept this part of life and utilize the tools they need to help, rather than destroy, intimacy.

I'm learning to stay in a difficult conversation rather than shut down or run away. I'm learning that some things don't get better unless I'm willing to be brave and deal with them.

Love your husband well by embracing conflict, refusing fear, and giving mutual respect as you share your thoughts with each other.

Father, help me walk through conflict rather than avoid it. Help me share my heart while I listen to his heart.

Dare learn what it takes to get through conflict to deeper intimacy. Dare use conflict to develop care and understanding of your spouse. In what ways will you get closer to him through conflict when it happens the next time?

_____

_____

_____

_____

_____

_____

_____

_____

_____

_____

Day 25

"The blind men came to him, and Jesus said to them, 'Do you believe that I am able to do this?'
They said to Him, 'Yes, Lord.' Then He touched their eyes, saying, 'According to your faith be it done to you.'"
Matthew 9:28&29

I wonder how many things these blind men had tried, how many of their loved ones wept and prayed for a remedy. I wonder how many women wished the men could see clearly and live a normal life.

Sister, what do you wish your man would see?

Jesus wants you to come to Him, and ask. If your man isn't coming to Christ for His need, Jesus invites you to bridge the gap and use your own spiritual authority to enter the throne room where all of heaven stands in holy awe of a working God.

In picturing the cross, realize when you bow before the cross, that the pole ascending vertically to the sky depicts your heart ascending to the throne. The arms extending horizontally to the world depicts your marriage. The arms of the cross are joined at the center, to the pole, which means your relationship with your man is joined to your own access to the throne room.

Focus on your upward relationship more than your horizontal relationship. The two of them are joined, and when the pole of the cross is firmly rooted to the ground, it extends upward without shaking. The arms, then, have a sturdy pole to be nailed to. Even so, your walk with God can pull your husband upward with power because any woman bowed before the cross of Jesus Christ becomes highly favored. All of heaven stands by in holy wonder at a prostrate heart lifted by the power of the cross rather than destroyed by earthly darkness.

Bow low today so that you can stand strong. Posture yourself in a place of inviting heaven's wonder and attention. Allow Jesus to ask, "'Do you believe that I am able to do this?'"

Are you willing to wait and, as you wait, to allow yourself to thrive—not just *survive*? Because when all of heaven stands over you, behind you, and before you, your inheritance is life in the face of death.

Father, I accept Your gift of thriving today. I believe that You are able to speak to my husband, but whether or not he listens, I invite heaven into my life as one who is highly favored by You.

Dare to live as one who is highly favored with all of heaven behind, before, and over your life! How will you posture yourself in God's favor today?

_____

_____

_____

_____

_____

_____

Day 26

Under three things the earth trembles; under four it cannot bear up: a slave when he becomes king, and a fool when he is filled with food; an unloved woman when she gets a husband, and a maidservant when she displaces her mistress. Proverbs 30:21–23

Women react in a variety of ways to the hurts in their lives. Some withdraw into a shell, others flaunt themselves, still others become controlling of their surroundings or people. Some hate themselves, others boast of their accomplishments to gain a sense of admiration. In any of the above cases, it is not pleasant to be around a woman who feels unloved.

Scripture says the Earth cannot bear up under an unloved woman who gets a husband. Feeling insecure, finally having a husband to whom she looks to for love, she controls him for a sense of importance and security. In him, she seeks to fill the sense of loss and expects him to fill her heart.

When he does not, she tries to change or fix the areas she thinks will make her feel better—and in the process, she unknowingly becomes the woman who tries to control her husband.

She does not fully realize, yet, how powerful the change of her heart will be when she looks to the Lord for gratification and love. Nor does she see how much it will quiet, calm, and bring beauty to her marriage.

Instead of grasping for love from her husband, she becomes an inviting lover. She becomes a freedom-giver. She becomes an asset to her man's life instead of a liability. In confidence she lives her life, lovable because she knows how much she is loved by God.

I believe our quest for love and security greatly diminishes the moment we realize how loved we already are. Share this loved place with your man more than grasping for a sense of worth from your man.

Father, more than grasp for love, help me to be an inviting lover.

Today, dare to quiet your restless heart even when you want to strive and grasp for the love you crave. Dare to simply accept love from your Father, then watch as it affects your earthly love. How will you find security in Christ today?

_____

_____

_____

_____

_____

_____

_____

_____

_____

_____

_____

Day 27

"If one gives an answer before he hears, it is his folly and shame." Proverbs 18:13

"So, I think I hear you say that you want to fix things around the house but you feel you don't have time, and you'd like me not to interpret that as a lack of love," I repeated back to my husband.

His face brightened quickly. "Yes!"

Because one of my love languages is quality time, and one of my natural gifts is managing time, I had been feeling unloved when my husband didn't take time to get things done for me sooner than he did. I figured that if he took time for some things but not for me, I was not near the top of his list.

"I'd like you to know that it's not a gauge of my love for you," he said. "I really feel like I don't have time to get things done—*but I love you.*"

We'd been going back and forth about the way the other made us feel. Neither one of us was feeling loved, and both were wanting understanding. I had listened to a podcast on reflective listening and realized that was what both of us were craving. Perhaps, rather than repeat what I thought he wasn't getting about me, I should repeat back what he wanted me to hear about his own heart.

Because when you hear a heart, you love a heart well. You don't have to agree with it, like it, or even approve of it—*but you must hear it well.* We must listen, then ask if we've heard correctly, then allow him to own his thoughts without being attacked for them. And before you panic, let me assure you that you can do this while still expressing your own need for him to consider. You simply learn to hear each other out more than shut each other up.

Lord, help me stop the cycle of trying to receive what I need before I'm able to listen reflectively. Help me to listen, repeat back to make sure I've understood, and allow him to own his thoughts.

Today's dare means we listen, really listen, to our man's words, then repeat back what we think he's trying to say and ask if it's correct. If it is, we accept it while still being honest with our own needs. How will you show your man you've heard him?

_____

_____

_____

_____

_____

_____

_____

_____

_____

_____

_____

_____

_____

Day 28

"But because of the temptation to sexual immorality, each man should have his own wife, and each woman her own husband. The husband should give to his wife her conjugal rights . . ." 1 Corinthians 7:2&3a

"I don't have a strong sex drive," she told me. "I just don't need it very often."

It's not surprising that some moms of little ones don't have sex at the top of their wish lists. There are also many women who were raped or abused and now have debilitating emotional trauma surrounding sexual intimacy. Then, there are others who are working through the feelings of betrayal because their husbands have broken their trust. A wife may feel sexually passionate for a while but tend toward apathy after years of marriage. Perhaps there are deep, unaddressed hurts in her relationship with her husband, a need for more nonsexual encounters, or simply a lack of drive in physical passion and desire. Whatever the case, struggling couples often refer to a lack of sex, and the reasons for it are as varied as the colors in the universe.

Another friend tells me, "I've met so many women who feel it's wrong to enjoy sexual pleasure." This one blows me away.

Dear sisters who've fed into this lie, do you ever wonder why your Creator designed your body to build up to ecstasy, then release into some of the best relaxation you could know? Why He made a part of your body to respond to touch with pleasure? Or why he created your man to want to see you enjoy this?

When it comes to marital sex, the most mature, Christlike thing we can do is let go and live it up! Give in to the womanly desire to be beautiful, and showcase yourself as much as you like! Grab hold of this: *sex is a gift!*

Dear sister who lives without orgasmic release, do you ever wonder why your heart feels less than satisfied, and your body pent up? Sexual pleasure is intended to draw you close to your man as few other things do, while relaxing your body more than an hour at the spa could. If you find yourself unable to get there, know that you are not alone—but know also that God's intention is for your body to be powerfully united to your husband's body, and He will give answers to bring you from a place of lack to one of overwhelming fullness.

Love your man well by embracing your body as God designed it. Embrace sexual joy even if you feel less than beautiful, less than ready, or less than equipped with all the knowledge you desire. Sex is a learning, growing, ever-increasing experience of pleasure and oneness with your man. Refuse to give the devil an inch at destroying it, and instead, keep inching forward into new and beautiful territory!

Father, thank You that what was stolen from many of us in a painful, destructive encounter can be washed away and replaced with joy in a beautiful sexual union with the man who truly loves us. Help us release all wrong done to us and fully embrace love given to us.

Today's dare is to grasp the fact that sex is a physical picture of everything we long for in Christ. When experienced with the man we love, it becomes an expression of love—mutual giving and receiving. In what ways can you make progress in this area?

Day 29

"May the God of hope fill you with all joy and peace in believing, so that by the power of the Holy Spirit you may abound in hope." Romans 15:13

There is beauty inside every single woman. Stifling it or refusing to recognize it is not an option if we want to be in a blessed marriage.

Beauty in spirit and body calls to the deepest core of who we are. And our men need our beauty more than we realize. We reclaim it when we realize that even our darkest hour may lead us to our greatest light.

Allowing life to rob us of beauty is tragic. That tender heart is meant for you to keep; the smile is meant to splash across your face. And if you decide to keep it, no one can take it.

Hurting woman who has let go of your beauty, reclaim it!

Sad woman who believes you have no beauty to offer: know that you do, and the best part of it is your joy. Cultivate every aspect of beauty you've been given.

Your man needs your smile to grace his life. He needs your joy to be worn on your face more than he needs you to wear the perfect outfit. He needs you to find, hold onto, and share with him the best places of your heart in spite of the worst places in your life. He needs you to find your greatest gifts and allow them to grow into a joyful outflow of your life. In short, he needs you to allow the best parts of you to grace your relationship.

Sometimes, in order to get to the beauty in our lives, we need to deal with the ugly parts of our lives. We need to deal with the hurts of our hearts so we can enjoy the best of our lives. Don't be afraid to enter a time of difficult soul healing, because in the end, you'll be able to enter a lifetime of soul joy. Deal with the hard things in your life so you won't turn into a hard person because of your life.

Your man needs you to fight the wars he cannot fight for you. He is human—not God—and he needs, most of all, for you to fight your wars with God rather than stand on the sidelines waiting for him to fight a war only God can fight for you.

Never forget whose you are, and for whom you live!

Father, forgive me for allowing life to rob me of beauty. Help me to reclaim it, and grace my marriage with it.

Today, make one dare—dare to reclaim your smile! In what ways will you allow God to fight your battles and grace your life with beauty?

_____
_____
_____
_____
_____
_____
_____

Day 30

"So if the Son sets you free, you will be free indeed."
John 8:36

She stood in my kitchen, this mother of five who had lost her husband just one year ago.

"I wish I had known about not giving in to self-pity when the kids were little," she said. "Mothering is hard work. I found myself withdrawing from my husband and not wanting to be near him. When he entered a room, I left the room. But one day, someone prayed against self-pity in my life, and I was set free. I went home and really *wanted* to be near my husband, hold his hand, and spend time with him."

She shook her head. She'd learned a lot over the years, and one of them was letting go.

Self-pity robs us of much and gives nothing in return. Self-pity takes our joy and shares no hope, help, or life. It steals what is rightfully ours, never gives, but takes even more away.

There's great difference between self-pity and self-help. One drowns you, the other lifts you to better things.

Pity refutes purpose and renders you useless, stripped, and bare. Refuse it, and reach for better things—including the things you need. Refuse to pity yourself, and purpose to help yourself, sometimes even by asking things from the man you love.

Father, help me to see that there is no purpose in pity.
Help me reach for what I need and be content with
what You see fit to provide.

Today's dare invites us to replace each pitying thought with a purposeful one. Dare not to wallow, but to hallow each thing God provides in your life. How will you move from self-pity to self-help today?

Day 31

"Let every person be quick to hear, slow to speak, slow to anger . . ." James 1:19b

One couple's story struck me. He had hurt her by ignoring her feelings while telling her what she should be feeling, instead. Then, he smiled at just the wrong time, and she took offense. The issue at hand was not small and she felt disregarded, then disrespected by his grin. Out of self-protection, she walked away.

Her man wasn't really laughing at *her;* he was smiling at the irony of their different views and how they could be so opposite. Telling her that, however, did little. The situation being discussed was ugly, and she wanted her feelings validated rather than to be told she just needed to find peace.

Some things are ugly no matter how much grace we find to walk through them, and sometimes we just need to be heard.

"I can't talk with him," she reasoned. "It never works. He doesn't know how to listen."

"I can't talk with her," he reasoned. "She can't stomach anything. She never hears me."

Truth was, they were both dealing with years of garbage, of which the smallest invocation flared into a blaze hotter than either of them knew what to do with.

She wrote him a text the next day: "I wanted to express that I'm ready to hear your heart whenever you're ready to share it. My goal will be to hear you and truly make you feel heard and give you a safe place to share your heart."

She was a smart woman to take note that not only she, but he as well, was feeling the same thing. Both of them just wanted to be heard. A strong person can give this before she gets it; only the weak refuse to do good before it's handed to them by another.

Professor Mehrabian says that communication is 7 percent verbal and 93 percent nonverbal. We listen with our countenance and body language even more than with our words. Look into your man's eyes with the love you want him to show when you need him to listen to you!

Lord, help us not to wait to extend the same kindness I wish to receive. Grant us the strength to give without expecting anything in return.

If your man frequently mentions that he's not being heard, dare head his way with a sincere apology. Remember that this does not imply you settle for less yourself—it does mean you are willing to give goodness because you know the Author of all things good. How will you humble yourself and pursue goodness today?

_____

_____

_____

_____

_____

_____

Day 32

"Or do you not know that your body is a temple of the Holy Spirit within you, whom you have from God? You are not your own." 1 Corinthians 6:19

I love seeing healthy, happy women whose lives are graced with good habits. When I see one, I observe her life, and each time I notice *freedom*. She cultivates her health, and this brings clarity to her life.

Cultivating health and beauty doesn't mean we have to be consumed with the latest fashions and fads. We don't feel pressure to look like Hollywood models or magazine cover girls. But it does mean we care for and represent ourselves in a way that honors the God Who created us. In doing so, we honor our husbands, as well.

We take note that our man's desire for physical beauty is not a small thing, and we spruce up for him. We purchase that lingerie and show it off at night. We care for our hair and wear clothing becoming to femininity. We do what it takes to stay fit and healthy. Ladies, our men don't need us to be a size two, but they truly do need us to care about and maintain our health. I believe that what our men are afraid of telling us, we need to tell each other. Their secret desire for beauty is often hidden by their greater desire not to hurt or offend us when we fail to maintain our bodies as well as possible.

We owe it to God, ourselves, our families, and our husbands to keep the beauty God gave us rather than allow it to be trashed by our own lack of discipline. I'm speaking boldly on this matter because I believe it deeply affects our joy and freedom.

It's hard to be truly happy when we're not healthy as a result of our own habits. It's difficult to be confident when we eat with guilt. But it's ultimately liberating to find emotional and physical health as a result of good habits we choose to implement in our daily lives. Let's bring the gift of confidence and health to our marriage!

Father, forgive me for not caring for the body You've given me. Please give me strength and persistence to reclaim my health.

Today, let's dare to do whatever it takes to get back on track with our health, knowing that God calls us to care for the body He's gifted us with. What steps will you take to change destructive habits?

_____

_____

_____

_____

_____

_____

_____

_____

_____

_____

Day 33

"For this very reason, make every effort to supplement your faith with virtue, and virtue with knowledge, and knowledge with self-control, and self-control with steadfastness, and steadfastness with godliness." 2 Peter 1:5–6

She was on cloud nine, writing her own Bible studies and teaching them, as well. For an entire year she wrote away, thrilled with the opportunity and alive with God's Spirit.

She waited for her man to be excited with her. But he never said a word—that is, not until she accidentally left a paper on the table that he assumed was left for him to critique. He gave it to her the next morning with red ink corrections.

She was devastated—and rightly so. We all love having our man's excitement and interaction with some great opportunity God brings our way. My friend's husband approved of her ministry but failed to verbalize it. Do you know what she said to me as she leaned over the table that day?

"I could have been wallowing in disappointment for days, but what an ugly place to live! I kept right on writing. God spoke to my heart that His delight is enough. I was already thrilled, having fun, excited, and God was in it with me. So I chose not to become bitter, but to keep allowing the *better* to work in my life."

This lady is one of the brightest women I know. Periodically I ask her out for lunch so I can glean from her wisdom. She's learned Whose she is, with Whom she's with, and for Whom she lives. From her spirit-awareness of God, her work becomes even more hallowed as she refuses to wallow.

One of the greatest gifts we give to our men is to cultivate our gifts. We do this whether or not our man coddles us when we want him to—we simply live out, to the best of our ability, what God put in. We allow personal joy to permeate relational aspects of life—and we never stop because of self-pity over something we didn't get that we expected to receive.

Lord, help us all to see that our husbands are not the deciding factor of our walks with You, and when they are being fully human, we still get to be fully alive in You.

Today's dare is not to wait around before you grasp your own spirit-awareness with God and all He's doing in you, through you, and for you. How will you release your man from needing to supply your heart needs perfectly?

_____

_____

_____

_____

_____

_____

_____

_____

Day 34

"And my God will supply every need of yours according to his riches in glory in Christ Jesus." Philippians 4:19

I stared at the tree line, silhouetted against a night sky, and my heart was filled with longing. I wanted to fix certain aspects of my marriage, and I didn't know how.

God spoke to me that night. I couldn't change another human being—not even my husband. And here I was, carrying the burden for both of us when God asked me to carry only mine. Because I was responsible for my own change, not his.

Because my husband will never be all I need, I get to release him and find joy. The same is true for him; neither of us will ever fill the greatest longing in the other, because our hearts were designed to need more than another human being. When we learn this, we are able to love each other and enjoy life together before every need is met.

God gives His gifts to bless our lives before we know how to function well in all aspects of our lives. He doesn't withhold His goodness from either of us until we find answers to the needs plaguing both of us. For this reason, a spouse can let go and let God, while enjoying the blessings of God in spite of existing needs.

God will supply your needs whether your man does or not. Do we see this? God desires all His daughters to look to *Him* more than to another human for their security, joy, and peace.

Follow Him with your own *yes*, and leave the rest to God. Say what He moves you to say; do what He prompts you to do. Speak truth and don't hide your needs. Simply know how to release your needs to a God Who promises to supply your soul richly.

Father, thank you for never leaving my soul empty, and for
giving me responsibility for myself alone.

Dare to live as a daughter whose birthright is one of boun-
ty. Claim all the riches of Christ today, and believe His
sure, spoken word to your heart. How will you follow
God to places of fullness?

Day 35

"For Your steadfast love is before my eyes, and I walk in Your faithfulness." Psalm 26:3

Have you ever heard of the difference between a desire and a goal? A desire is often contingent on another and can leave you dissatisfied, whereas a goal gives you profitable things to strive for.

A goal for better communication with your husband will help you pave the way for the desire to be realized.

Rather than fret about what your husband isn't changing (perhaps even after you've let him know what you need), turn your deep desires into goals and begin doing profitable things to meet them. While you communicate honestly with your man about your needs, begin walking toward your goal on your own.

If you feel alone in your quest for better communication, know that when you change your own negative ways of relating to your man, this gives him an entirely different person to relate to. Know that you may well be the one to pave the way. If you have a burning desire for change, God will most likely give you viable tools to use because He wants to see your desires met.

If you look back on your communication style and realize you've been defensive, accusatory, and argumentative, take a step back and change. Give your spouse someone different to relate to.

If I listen to my husband's heart rather than become offended by his words; if I ask him what he's truly experiencing and would like me to know; and if I then offer empathy, communication problems have a greater chance at being solved.

Love your man well by listening well!

Lord, help me be strong enough to allow my husband to express his heart without fear of getting silent treatment or an angry response in return.

Today, dare show your strength by listening to what your man needs to express, but may be afraid to say. Dare ask him, and allow him to speak without fear. What will you do to show your husband that you're hearing him?

_____

_____

_____

_____

_____

_____

_____

_____

_____

_____

_____

_____

_____

_____

Day 36

"Blessed are the pure in heart, for they shall see God."
Matthew 5:8

Our men need us to be modest in our actions and pure in our hearts. One of the best ways to love your man is by staying pure for him.

A pure heart cannot help but display pure actions.

A modest woman feels no need to display her body inappropriately for attention from men. She has no need to be gratified with another man's eyes on her in a lustful way. She is happy to simply be a friend, a sister who is a true blessing. She will care about the way she dresses and will do her best to avoid inappropriate displays of her body.

Discretion to her is not a chore; it is her desire. Dare be one of those women who is appreciated for her modest beauty rather than lusted over for an inappropriate display of her body.

How do you react to the man who is unashamedly interested in you, though you are a married woman? Do you enjoy it, hanging around and chatting for more attention, or do you run in the opposite direction, whatever that may mean in your situation?

Graciously accepting a compliment or appreciating a friendship is healthy and good, but our men need to know that our hearts are always with them, and only them. They need to be able to trust us on our phones, social media, or in public. They need to know we wouldn't say anything on a screen that we would not say to a real person while standing in front of our husbands. Let's love our men well by living a trustworthy life!

Lord, help me be trustworthy and allow only healthy relationships in my life. Help me use wisdom while knowing what to embrace and what to shun.

Today, if you have an unhealthy friendship, dare to run fast even if you want to stay long. Dare to open your heart to your man rather than shut down on your man. Is there anything you need to change in order to give your heart more fully to your husband?

_____

_____

_____

_____

_____

_____

_____

_____

_____

_____

_____

_____

_____

Day 37

"By wisdom a house is built, and by understanding it is established." Proverbs 24:3

Can we talk?" I asked my husband.

The look on his face was as if I had asked him to build me a new house in the middle of a snowstorm. And of course, I felt less than loved, immediately.

A group of people once laid a baby girl down and watched where her eyes would focus. They immediately focused on, and held the gaze of, the eyes hovering over her. Then, they laid a baby boy down. His eyes looked into their faces, then immediately drifted to the ceiling fan, where they stayed focused on the moving object.

Even a baby girl wants to connect, continue connecting, and hold the connection. As she grows, she will want this whether or not things are smooth in her relationship. When things are messy, she will confront the mess to remove it—*but her man may well think she is attacking him, instead.*

When men think we are confronting to control, we are most likely confronting to connect. We want to look into his face, have him look into ours, and peel back layers of our hearts for him to see—even if the problem is *him.*

This is good. But if our men don't listen well at the moment, or want to talk, it is vital that we understand why. They often feel threatened by the fact that we think something is wrong with *them.* That we are unhappy with *them.* That we think they have needs and we have what it takes to fix *them.*

How about coming to him with your needs, but using *I* statements rather than *you* statements? "I'm feeling . . ." will come across as less agressive than "You always . . ."

In these words, you have a voice, but you use it in ways that will make it easier for him to hear you out and rise to meet your need. If he is a kind man, you pull the provider instinct forth rather than the defending one.

Lord, help me not to bottle up, but to communicate well. Give me wisdom on how to share my heart without attacking my husband's heart. Help him see my heart to connect, and do what it takes to get us there.

Today, dare to express your needs with a focus on your needs rather than attacking him for making you feel a certain way. Dare to be both honest and honoring!

_____

_____

_____

_____

_____

_____

_____

_____

_____

Day 38

"You will not need to fight in this battle. Stand firm, hold your position, and see the salvation of the Lord on your behalf, O Judah and Jerusalem. Do not be afraid and do not be dismayed. Tomorrow go out against them, and the Lord will be with you." 2 Chronicles 20:17

Part of loving your husband well is learning how to shed codependency.

Codependents find it easier to forgive than to stand up in the face of ongoing wrong. Something about their own strength terrifies them because they are dependent on the strength of others. This is why they go down with whatever happens around them.

If this is you, you must see that your value goes much deeper than keeping someone else happy and at bay. You are not a victim. Nor are you responsible for things beyond your control.

Many women silently endure years of abuse or sexual betrayal, often in the form of pornography. Because of the secrecy of the betrayal, they suffer silently while trying to regain what was lost. If they don't stand strong against the destructive behavior, their own emotions go down. A wife in this place must reach out and get the help they both need just as someone would with an actual physical affair. Your hurt and anger are there because actions on a screen are also unfaithfulness.

A man respects a woman with boundaries. And if he wants her, he will stay with her and be faithful to her in both hidden and obvious ways. If he doesn't, you won't be happy with him if you've "begged" him into faithfulness. His heart will still wander unless it's remade.

Women, you must speak up and you must speak out. Sometimes, if he does not repent with true change, you must also walk out. Respect and honor is not silently enduring wrong without a voice. Respect calls forth the respectable and doesn't hesitate to shun dishonorable behavior. Unfaithfulness, domestic violence, and pornography (which is a form of unfaithfulness) are all things you need not tolerate and have every right to shun.

Christian woman—your man, your marriage, and your own heart need you to stand strong against sin!

Father, help me realize that my identity is not tied up in my husband to the point of living below human dignity. Help me reclaim my right as Your daughter.

Today, let this be the last day you leave places open for the enemy to trample. Dare draw your lines, and make them clear. How will you be strong today?

_____

_____

_____

_____

_____

_____

Day 39

"And you will know the truth, and the truth will set you free." John 8:32

Love your husband well by giving him freedom.

I often comment on another woman's beauty to alleviate any awkwardness he may feel in the moments he cannot help but notice another woman. That girlish (and immature) desire to be the only beautiful woman to my husband has been replaced by the reality that there are many, many beautiful women in the world.

Healthy acknowledgment sheds light on the heart and freedom in the soul while staying within proper boundaries.

The truth, even if it is opposes our natural desires, always sets us free to live in a healthier way.

If my husband feels he cannot acknowledge and appreciate beauty in a healthy, nonsexual way, I believe it brings bondage and guilt where none is due. The same is true for us ladies. We cannot force ourselves to believe certain men are not handsome and attractive. There should be no guilt on either you or your husband for acknowledging truth to yourselves.

Releasing your heart to acknowledge what is pure will enable you to better gain victory over things that are not pure. In an effort to "keep your husband pure," you can throw so much bondage on him that it becomes even more difficult for him to stay pure.

You don't need to be on top in order to feel secure. You don't need to be the most beautiful woman in the room in order to know you are loved. Your man needs you to release expectations that are not in line with truth, and give him grace to be real. He needs you to allow him to notice and appreciate beauty without being accused of sin—*because it's not sin!*

Lord, help me to love my husband well by not dumping guilt on him for things beyond his control. Help me gift him with freedom to live in truth in all areas of life.

If your man feels squelched in this area and constantly fears your insecure outbursts over things that are not wrong, dare go to him, today. What will you do to free the air your husband breathes?

Day 40

"Give, and it will be given to you. Good measure, pressed down, shaken together, running over, will be put into your lap. For with the measure you use it will be measured back to you." Luke 6:38

In order to love your man well, you need to allow him to love you well.

Sometimes we know more about leaning into others' brokenness than we do about sharing our own. Living as though we are angels rather than needy humans makes us so weary we end up being even more needy.

Allow him to serve you, and you will serve him better.

I had to learn that it was OK to have my husband sacrifice for me. The more I became honest with my own needs, the more my needs were cared for. I had to learn that it was OK to inconvenience him.

Treating yourself as having little value is not in line with God's thoughts of you. When I learned to ask things of my husband, he greatly appreciated knowing what I needed rather than being confused with my vacillating performance and emotional upsets.

Because when you hide your true self, you end up breaking in ugly ways. You carry around the baggage of your broken, exhausted, performing self. You perform for a while, then your true colors spill. You confuse others with differing statements—one of them your true thoughts, the other, the thing you say to gain approval after you think you've lost it.

Honesty cannot happen only once; honesty is a lifestyle.

The pressure of being responsible for everyone's happiness can cause you to break. You'll fall apart while your man *remains clueless of your need because you are doing so well at covering your soul in a pitiful attempt to love or be loved.*

Love your husband well by paying attention to your own needs and allowing him to help meet them.

God, help us to see that our men do not benefit from us striving to be everything. Help us to be the one thing they truly need—wives walking by their side with needs of our own, mutually giving and receiving.

Today, dare make a request for the one thing you need or desire more than anything else in your relationship. What need will you express to your husband today?

Day 41

"Whoever brings blessing will be enriched . . ."
Proverbs 11:25

I'm walking the grocery aisles again, wondering how much money to spend and how much to save. Truth is, I'm not a foodie—but a few of my family members are! I pull the fancy lunch meat off the shelf and place it in the cart.

After a full day, I realize my husband's schedule has changed, and he's leaving early in the morning. I don't have his usual lunch packed, but it's late and the kids need to get to bed. "You don't need to pack it," he tells me. "I'll figure something out."

I shake my head. "I want to pack it." I'm heading for the shower, then heading for the kitchen, where I start spreading mayonnaise at 10:30 p.m. He and the kids chat around me while I work, and before long the lunch is in the fridge for his early day.

I don't always do this. Life is real and sometimes I allow him to sacrifice for me. But ladies, where are our men on the priority list? Are their needs important to you, or do you shrug them off quickly with some sort of annoyance at another interruption in your day?

If I hadn't wanted to serve my husband well, I would not have placed the meat in the cart to begin with but would have prioritized my money-saving desires. I didn't know he needed a quick lunch the next day, but God did. When our hearts are in tune with God's, he works out our service.

Our kids need us to love on their father more than they need us to be everything for them at all times. Even the kids need us to keep our man our priority. Though this looks different for each marriage, a giving heart can be sensed more than seen. You can have a giving heart even while needing to say no at times—just make sure you say yes many times!

True love is marked with sacrifice; love him well by serving him when it costs you.

Father, forgive us for viewing our husbands as one more need in the day rather than one of the top priorities of our day.

Today, dare say no to something so you can say yes to your man. How will you go out of your way to serve him today?

_____

_____

_____

_____

_____

_____

_____

_____

_____

_____

_____

Day 42

"If the Lord had not been my help, my soul would soon have lived in the land of silence." Psalm 94:17

My son and his little friend had fought a lot that day on the lake. On the way home, my friend and I demanded utter silence from them because our heads had been ringing with unwanted conflict for most of the afternoon. We turned on the music and drove quietly—because sometimes, little boys happen on such a mood that if a single word escapes their lips, it is ugly.

Silence is better than ugly, but *silence is not better than joy.*

As we drove in silence, I watched other ladies facing my car when we all paused at the red light. The first looked as if she'd been crying; the second, as if she knew the weight of the world would rest on her shoulders as soon as she reached her destination.

And I wondered, where was the joy—for all of us ladies?

If God had not released my own heart, I'd be in silence somewhere behind the bars of condemnation, guilt, and fear. But He said to me as He said to Lazarus that day (John 11:43), "Sara, come forth!"

He broke my old chains and called me out. Out of silence into giving life; out of guilt into freedom; out of fear into faith; out of despair into joy; out of codependence into confident living.

He calls you out, too. And your marriage is waiting for you to be called out, to speak out, to live in joy.

What is gripping you? Of what are you afraid? What clutches at your neck each day, blocking the joy you want to inhale? If you think another person is stifling your joy, you are wrong. Because the power of the cross is greater

than another sinful human, and the breath you get to receive from the Spirit of Christ is a greater inhalation of life
than the other finite lives you want to depend on. Those
lives have no power to give a single breath, but God created you and the air you breathe. Depend on Him, and you'll
be filled by Him!

God, please break my soul out of silence
and help me to breathe in joy!

Today, dare break the chains that silence you. Ask God
to call you out of darkness and into light. What's holding
you back from experiencing God's joy for you and your
marriage?

_____

_____

_____

_____

_____

_____

_____

_____

Day 43

"But Godliness with contentment is great gain."
1 Timothy 6:6

My husband and I will never be one of those "perfect" couples who rise each morning for coffee and time together before the day begins. Our life is sporadic, unpredictable, and crazy.

My husband needs me to release expectations so he can accomplish a life of real sacrifice in his law enforcement world. And by doing so, I am free.

I do not want to be bound to anything but love in my marriage. If we are bound to circumstances, we are no longer free to love without perfection in our circumstances. And if we need perfection in our circumstances, we need to acknowledge that we are not governed by love, but by a selfish impulse to gratify our own hearts in the name of love.

I deeply admire all military wives who say good-bye to their men for months or years at a time. They've released most every expectation there is to have—and they're still there because they are good women who see that the world revolves around more than their own ups and downs.

Our men need us to be brave. Brave isn't fun when what you really want is ease. But when we are gripped with expectations, they will often be unmet, and we join the ranks of women who will never be satisfied. Be brave enough to accept that life is an adventure full of ups and downs. When we let go of our own expectations of perfection, we make room for God to move in our lives and marriages.

Lord, please help me release unrealistic expectations and learn to find joy. Help me experience contentment by trusting Your ways are better than my ways.

Today, dare to accept your life, your late dinner, your month without a date, your cranky kids. Then, see what kind of joy you can create right in the midst of your very real life! How can you embrace reality today, and find joy in it?

Day 44

"Who redeems your life from the pit, who crowns you
with steadfast love and mercy." Psalm 103:4

Our men need us to allow them to fail.

Yes, fail. Or even sin, or have gaping needs and flaws . . .
Loving your man is entirely different from loving his need
(which you may always hate, by the way, no matter how
much you love *him*).

As one man puts it, "I don't want her to just love me, I
want her to *be in love with me.*"

When you're truly in love with your man, you don't
expect him to be sinless or faultless so that you can love
him. *You just love him.*

The perfection of Christ will never be fully realized
through imperfect people. If we base our experience of an
Infinite Creator on a finite creation, we will be disappoint-
ed, and in danger of never fully experiencing grace.

*We need Perfect Love more than we need perfect husbands.
More than we need our man to treat us perfectly, we need to
know what it's like to be perfectly loved by God.* Free living
happens when we are no longer bound to expectations
of perfection and learn that love triumphs because love is
greater.

When we are governed by love, we are readily embraced
by that love.

Embrace your own journey. Accept his imperfection. He
is in need, just like you. There are reasons for his behavior,
just as there are reasons for your own. And only a good
God Who invites us to draw from the well of salvation is
able to heal and save us all.

God, I choose to love my husband right where he is. I choose to love him when he fails me and when he doesn't.

Today's dare is to accept that you are married to a human being living a real life, who will fail you in real ways. Hollywood can create perfection on a screen, but this Earth will only boast of real men with real needs. How will you dare to love—and even better, dare to *be in love*?

Day 45

"Fear not, stand firm, and see the salvation of the Lord, which he will work for you today." Exodus 14:13a

The lady whose story I read broke me.

Her husband was flirting, hanging out with, and inappropriately engaging with a neighbor woman while disrespecting his wife. Of course, it was all justified in that "there's nothing going on," and she was made to feel guilty for her discomfort.

She was allowing herself to be used in an unjust manner. He had no respect for her in part because she didn't respect herself enough to stand up to him. Her friends asked her, "Why do you let him do this to you?" to which she replied, "I'm not 'letting him.' I'm suffering because he's doing it."

Codependents are always victims because they don't see how they can help themselves.

This dear lady may not be able to change him, but she could remove herself. She could quickly get counsel and know she is not caught, stuck under his roof while he brings home the neighbor woman. She could tell him how his behavior is hurting her and demand an honest explanation. If there's really nothing going on, he shouldn't mind talking about it to clear up the confusion. If there is something going on that shouldn't be, she has every right to set boundaries to protect her own heart. And if he's unwilling to let go of the other girl, she could remove herself from him until he is willing to be a one-woman man.

She could be proactive rather than drowning in her emotions and becoming even more of a doormat for her selfish husband to walk over.

If you're a wife whose husband has ongoing unfaithfulness issues, refuse to ignore the situation. Give your husband a choice—you or other women—but don't force yourself to put up with his lifestyle as if nothing were wrong.

Whether your abuse is physical or emotional, refuse to stand by silently. You will only add years to your grief and prolong the problem. You must speak up. He will end his problem much sooner if you stand up to him than if you keep false peace that leads to disaster.

Your man needs to know you have boundaries just as he needs to know you love him. He needs to know this even if he's healthy and has never sinned against you in this area. But he desperately needs you to have boundaries if he's weak or has already failed you in these areas. You are never meant to suffer alone. If you think you are, you have a debilitating view of leadership and submission. You can be set free!

Father, help me not to live with sins that destroy my well-being. Show me how to stand, and how to remove myself if my husband doesn't remove his sin.

Today, dare to know that you need not live in the midst of unfaithfulness for one more day. Dare give your husband a choice, then dare follow through on what you've said. How will you learn to stand in love for what is right?

Day 46

"With joy you will draw water from the wells of salvation. And you will say in that day: 'Give thanks to the Lord, call upon his name, make known his deeds among the peoples, proclaim that his name is exalted.'"
Isaiah 12:3&4

Holding in your true feelings results in distance from your spouse. A close, happy marriage is always real. When you are not real, you may well end up bottling it up, then blowing it up!

Those who give most thanks are happier, and also most comfortable expressing grief or concern to their spouse. If you don't hold in the appreciation, you won't need to hold in the grievances.

Wanting to please our man is a good thing; however, we don't really please him when we are not sharing who we really are.

Men love a woman who reasons and ponders things of importance. Good men are not drawn to doormats.

What matters is your heart of respect. Are you able to express yourself in a way that makes him feel respected? Does he feel threatened with your attitude when you communicate? Never bottle things up, but share your inside feelings with your man to create loving dialogue.

Create a bedrock of thanksgiving and appreciation for your man and you'll be able to communicate grievances to your man even better!

Lord, help me not to bottle things up. Help me share my heart in honesty and truth.

Today's dare leads you to reach out and express that heart of yours in an honest, real, and altogether respectable manner. How will you build a foundation of appreciation for your man?

_____
_____
_____
_____
_____
_____
_____
_____
_____
_____
_____
_____
_____
_____
_____
_____
_____
_____
_____

Day 47

"Bear one another's burdens, and so fulfill the law of
Christ." Galatians 6:2

My husband is a cop—strong, buff, and brave. And
when I married him, he was preaching and, in my mind,
had the answers to most of life.

In some abstract, idolizing way that didn't embrace his
humanity, I'd been living as if he didn't need the same kind
of heart care that I needed, that he could handle anything,
and I could pretty much be full of need because he was my
constant supply. Simply put, I was an idolizing, codependent wife.

Talk about draining a man. It took time to learn that he
wasn't infallible and he did, indeed, have limits.

I'm learning that he needs to be heard as much as I
do. Because people are people, and your husband's heart,
though very different from yours, is still a heart.

I'm listening better, empathizing more, *hearing him out
rather than shutting him out.* And I'm baffled as to why we
women expect our marriages to thrive under attitudes and
words we don't even expect our friends to put up with.

Today, no matter how difficult your conversation or
how much you disagree, dare lean toward your man rather
than stiffen away from him. Listen well and disagree with
respect, just as you would if you were talking with your
friends.

Honoring your man doesn't imply letting go of your
own honor; it actually implies that your own is so well
established that you know how to share it with your man.
Share it with him, and care for his heart as your share your
heart!

God, help me to lean in toward my man when we disagree.
Help me honor his heart even when I differ with his ideas or
opinions.

Today, dare treat your man with the same (or more) courtesy and respect you show your friends, boss, or acquaintances. What tones or attitudes will you stop today, and how will you replace them with better ones?

_____

_____

_____

_____

_____

_____

_____

_____

_____

_____

_____

_____

_____

_____

_____

_____

Day 48

"The Lord your God is in your midst, a Mighty One Who will save; He will rejoice over you with gladness; He will quiet you by His love; He will exult over you with loud singing." Zephaniah 3:17

When the inaugural cruise for Focus on the Family began, staff on the ship gave the initial instructions on what to do if the ship went down. "Women and children first!" they called out.

Not a single feminist protested or called the staff sexist. Not one of them ran forward declaring herself as willing to give her life as the men. And the men, well, they stood like soldiers wearing orange life vests, ready to die for their women.

Though our roles as men and women are equally important, they are different.

If we were the same, we'd be out fighting wars as much as the men are. And if men were equally capable of the same things as we, they would be just as adept at things women are best at doing. They'd prefer shopping to hunting and enjoy lattes over black coffee.

Men are men and women are women because the world needs both, and it needs both desperately. Some things are never meant to change and will remain as they are no matter how long and hard we try to change them.

We are created, sisters. Being created in a certain way is a gift, and one to live to the fullest. We cannot live our own gifts well if we fight for another's. There is simply not enough energy for both.

You have nothing to become, nothing to prove—*only everything womanly to be*—and that may look different for various women. One may enjoy hunting bear alongside her man while another cringes at shooting a duck. Being who you already are is much more productive than trying to become someone you were never created to be. Dare be the woman you were meant to be in spite of the fact that some men are not the men they are called to be.

Realizing that your own actions need not be determined by the actions of another is a true, productive understanding of control!

Lord, help us realize that healing from our hurts comes from allowing You to heal us and walking in all the grace You offer us. Help us release the inner need to control men in order to prove ourselves.

Today, dare honor your man even though you've been hurt by men (and perhaps your own man). How will you release control today and learn, instead, to allow God's peace to reign in your heart?

_____

_____

_____

_____

_____

_____

Day 49

"Train the young women to love their husbands and children, to be self controlled, pure, working at home, kind, and submissive to their own husbands, that the word of God may not be reviled." Titus 2:4&5

The difference between men and women has nothing to do with levels of importance, significance, or greatness. It has nothing to do with fairness. It does have everything to do with the fact that God created men to function well in a certain manner, and they cannot help it. They are walking in divine order.

We often attribute a man's actions to attitude rather than constitution. Ask yourself, "Is it okay for him to need respect even though it's different from my own need for love?"

How often are we frustrated, attributing his actions to some need rather than realizing this is in his very make-up as a man? *We want him to understand and accept us, minister to us in the way we receive love, but how are we relating to his needs and inborn tendencies?* How are we appreciating that the very nature that makes him willing to die for us is the same nature needing respect?

Perhaps next time he offers advice when all we want is to be held, we can break down and laugh instead of rise up in anger. Or next time we get lost and he doesn't want to pull over and ask for directions, we can smile instead of seethe. Maybe when he wants to take on that challenge, rather than try to tame him into a perfect American family lifestyle, we can follow in his wild pursuit of *conquering the wilderness.*

We may well end up much happier in that wilderness (whatever it is) than we would be pushing that stroller down the sidewalk of our modern suburb with a restless man at our side.

A man's need for respect is not prideful. God created him to lead just as He created you to be loved.

The very qualities that first draw us to a man are often the things that bother us most after living life together for a while. We begin to resent what we should rejoice in, to grasp for what we should give, to require what we should make requests for. Loving our man well means we embrace his constitution without condemnation.

Father, help me to accept and embrace the different ways we were created by You, for Your purpose and for Your world.

Today, dare to fully accept your man's constitution. Dare to embrace the differences between you two, and only label things as selfish when they truly are. How will you respond to his manhood today?

_____

_____

_____

_____

_____

_____

Day 49

For the wife does not have authority over her own body,
but the husband does. Likewise the husband does not
have authority over his own body, but the wife does."
1 Corinthians 7:3&4

*It is an absolute honor to fill the sexual need in your man's
life.* Being desired with passion should awaken us to give
with abandon.

God designed a man's body to need sexual release almost as much as he needs food. Just as we cannot help
certain bodily functions of our own, so he cannot help his
drive.

Many women attribute a man's endless desire for sex
to some selfish mechanism he could help if he really cared
about her needs. After all, she is so tired when she finally
hits the pillow. She loses out on the honor he shows when
he wants to make love. She ceases to appreciate that being
desirable to a man means she is a lovely part of his life. She
turns him off, and many times, away.

She forgets that his biological drive may create strong
temptations the next day at work.

And if he cheats, the world will hear as she files for
divorce papers. *But will the world hear about her lack as a
woman to understand her man and make it one of her chiefest
prerogatives to make him glad?*

I'm not advocating that women are to blame if their
men cheat—never! Some men are unfaithful no matter
what a woman does—and even if you've failed to be there
for him, you are not to blame for his sin. But if you want
to love your man well, you will strive to meet his sexual
need well. If there are roadblocks hindering your abandon, by all means pay attention to your heart and care for

it, realizing that you are just as important a part in your sexual experience, and your freedom is crucial for healthy intimacy. Forcing yourself is not healthy—giving and receiving sexual pleasure is! A kind man will gladly abstain if his wife needs a period of time for healing, and a loving woman will gladly do what it takes to ensure a healthy sex life in her marriage.

This is a sensitive topic, with many men in sexual need while many women live with emotional need. If you need help resolving underlying issues, reach out humbly and vulnerably, so that sexual intimacy and pleasure can be a gift that keeps on giving—to both of you.

Father, help me shed anything today that would hinder me truly wanting to know what love looks like to my husband.

Dare to grow this gift! How can you remove obstacles of sexual enjoyment between you and your husband?

_____

_____

_____

_____

_____

_____

Day 50

"Beloved, let us love one another, for love is from God, and whoever loves has been born of God and knows God. Anyone who does not love does not know God, because God is love." 1 John 4:7&8

I noticed the pots of randomly planted greenery as I walked across her porch. She loved minigardens, and spent hours placing multiple things into one pot to create a masterpiece of beauty. And as we worked together, this is what she told me:

"Nature is at war with our idea of beauty. Nature loves diversity. We try to create beauty the human way, symmetrically lining up the same things. The same is true in marriage—you cannot fix your husband into the same copy of yourself. If you try, one of you will break. You cannot fix him any more than you want him to fix you."

Her husband pulled in as I was leaving, and she lit up. Something about her reminded me of a newlywed bride in love. They were of polar opposite personalities—she, bubbly as a fountain, and he as quiet as the mountains surrounding their home—but it was clear that she *loved him.*

I'm guessing she could have been griping about some difference in him that she'd love to change. He probably doesn't communicate as much as she wishes he would. But she's learned to enjoy love more than gripe about a certain aspect of their relationship.

I pulled away with a smile splashing my face because it was refreshing and completely adorable. In allowing her man to be who he was, she released herself to enjoy love in the many ways it showed itself.

Father, forgive me for thinking that marriage needs to line up with all my ideas of love. Help me, instead, to simply be in love.

Today, dare release your man to be the best version of himself. Express your needs, but don't force him to line up to your ideas. How can you appreciate your man for who he is and what he already does for you?

Day 51

"Do not let your adornment be merely outward—arranging the hair, wearing gold, or putting on fine apparel—rather let it be the hidden person of the heart, with the incorruptible beauty of a gentle and quiet spirit, which is very precious in the sight of God." 1 Peter 3:3–4, NKJV

Just as every woman desires beauty, every man wants to be honored and respected. *Ladies, our walk with the Lord speaks little or nothing to our men unless they feel respected.* Without it, outer beauty soon loses its appeal and grace while our "spirituality" seems not so spiritual at all.

Christian women are prone to rejoice in grace while remaining unaware of the tools they need to show that grace to their families. The Lord is asking us to walk in respect just as He is asking us to walk in peace, forgiveness, love, or any other fruit of the Spirit.

Many women focus on friendships and ministry when they have a hurting husband who does not feel respected. *This is like trying to go to bed at night when we have not yet faced the morning.* It is counterproductive, and yes, even destructive.

What a shame that women say they love Jesus (and wish their husband did as well) but do not see the power of respect and a Godly life. What a shame when they nag and talk, instead of building up their husband's heart and showing him what true, agape love looks like.

Speak in love, but if there is no response, walk your walk more than you talk your talk. Above all, make sure your walk lines up with your talk!

Lord, help me make my marriage an even greater priority than ministry, work, or kids. Help me do what it takes to walk in honor.

Today, dare to leave the rest of your life second in line while you begin focusing on your man's loneliness and lack. How will you change his lack of feeling respected to a state of having what he needs?

Day 52

"May the God of endurance and encouragement grant
you to live in such harmony with one another, in accord
with Christ Jesus, that together you may with one voice
glorify the God and Father of our Lord Jesus Christ."
Romans 15:5&6

We pulled up to the ferry dock and sat waiting in the
small blue car, when she looked over at me and asked, "Do
all men need the same things?"

We had been talking the whole long way, this talented
lady who was headed to another one of her book signings,
and I along to learn.

"I got married with no clue about how to relate to
men," she continued. "I took my best shot in the dark. I
wish I had known."

I nodded my head. I felt the same way. What if we could
do it all over again without making the same mistakes? We
hadn't always known how to pull the best out of the men
we married.

We didn't know (or didn't live like we knew) that con-
tinuous expressed disappointment causes a man to feel
defeated, whereas expressed trust causes him to feel responsibility. Our best shots in the dark hadn't always cut it
when it came to touching the hearts of our men.

Did you know that expressing trust in a man often causes him to want to do the very thing most women nag at
him to do? Though we are not responsible for his lack
when he fails us, we greatly add to his discouragement and
lack of desire to please us when we express constant disappointment.

Learn to express your thoughts honestly, and to share
your ideas, needs, and desires without nagging. If need be,

debate him without disrespecting him. You are not a door-mat—but neither should you be a dripping faucet! Let go of grievances after they have been expressed, and focus instead on a lifestyle of building him up.

Father, help me express encouragement and trust to my husband in all the ways I can honestly do so.

If you habitually complain, dare close your lips when there's another opportunity to complain, then express trust or appreciation for something, instead. How will you be honest with your needs without nagging?

_____

_____

_____

_____

_____

_____

_____

_____

_____

_____

Day 53

"It is better to live in a corner of the housetop than in a house shared with a quarrelsome wife." Proverbs 21:9

When a man's heart wants something, everyone knows it. The world oooohs and aaaahs when his heart is geared toward a woman in tenderness. We all love the story of Romeo and Juliet, and I haven't ceased to be intrigued with Wallace in *Braveheart* when his heart so longed after his beloved. The world over, women sigh with longing while unknowingly stifling the very fire they try to flame.

Would that we knew what the male gender wished we knew. Thankfully, there is wisdom for those of us willing and eager to learn.

Today, focus on doing practical things to deepen your connection with your man. If your man's love language is acts of service, do something out of the norm for him today. If it is words of affirmation, tell him something specific you appreciate about him. If it is touch, load up the back rub, holding hands, or sexual intimacy.

Ladies, we can awake our men or we can stifle our men. We can badger them or we can boost them. We can kindle their love or throw water on the hottest flames.

A wise woman will encourage the best parts of her man's heart instead of badgering him for more while at the same time draining his heart with her words and actions.

Father, help me to boost my man more than badger him; to kindle his love rather than dampen his fire.

Dare to do or say something that will make your man come alive. Consider one thing, then bravely do it! What will it be?

_____

_____
_____
_____
_____
_____
_____
_____
_____
_____
_____
_____
_____
_____
_____
_____
_____
_____
_____
_____
_____

Day 54

"For to us a child is born, to us a son is given; and the government shall be upon his shoulder, and his name shall be called Wonderful, Counselor, Mighty God, Everlasting Father, Prince of Peace." Isaiah 9:6

Have you ever had violent emotional feelings about some current circumstance or person and wondered how your heart could take over so strongly over something seemingly small?

I have. Many times, actually.

You may wonder why you're not able to handle something another woman handles well. Why you cry for hours over one small fight with your husband. Why you fly off the handle when your children fight. Why you have massive feelings of rejection when someone says something nasty about you.

You may feel defeated, frustrated, or insecure about yourself. Probably guilty. You want to do better, perform well.

Then it happens again. You crash over some minor incident. Perhaps people label you "needy" or something else that makes you feel low. You retreat to the only safe place you know, and that is inward. If you stay alone you will be safe. But alone is lonely.

Trying to perform better is like trying to hide a nasty infection under a piece of paper. The paper will become soiled and soak into the oozing wound. Quite soon it will be no covering at all.

You must look deeper. Looking deeper takes time, bravery, and effort. It takes vulnerability and wisdom from others. It takes humility.

Loving your man well includes taking care of inner turmoil. Though some of your wounds may be caused even by him, he can remain clueless of the inner turmoil of your heart if you are not willing to look deeply and honestly. Love him well by finding answers for your need so that you are free—free to give, free to receive.

Father, I let go of performance for the sake of peace, and I resolve to get to true peace. Please help me know and understand what is going on.

Today, dare to get real, deep, and honest. Dare to go places that frighten you. Dare be vulnerable with your heart to those who can help your heart. Who will you seek help from in your journey to wholeness?

_____

_____

_____

_____

_____

_____

_____

_____

_____

$\mathcal{D}ay$ 55

"In quietness and in trust shall be your strength."
Isaiah 30:15b

Have you ever found yourself crying inconsolably over something that seems minor? Or feel anger boiling up inside after a relatively small offense? Maybe you're just overtired or hormonal. Or maybe there are deeper wounds to be healed.

Do not try to "fix" everything so you can be happy. Ask God what unhealed or unresolved problem lies within you to cause your reaction. When He shows you, take serious time and prayer to heal it. Ask for help. Whatever the case, find relief for your own sake and the sake of your loved ones.

When the train of your emotions begins rushing down the track, get out of the way. Step aside, watch, and wait. Stay calm. God has a better way than for you to go under.

Hurting people hurt people. But healed people also release people and bring freedom to those around them. Find inner healing today, and use the strength of your emotions to help you understand that something deeper is going on. By rewiring your thoughts, you can prevent another fall into the holes you've experienced in life. Those around you need not suffer from your pain anymore.

We think we need to "do" something differently when most times God just wants to help us "be" different, be healed, be made whole. Performing and being healed are two very different things. The former will render you superficial and less than warm toward your man, while the latter will release your heart to experience the peace you long for.

Father, help me to see that healing is the only thing that will make me truly whole, which in turn changes the way I handle life from the inside out.

Today, dare take a deeper look to see why relatively small things cause debilitating turmoil in your heart. What does God need to uncover so that your heart can be healed?

Day 56

"So teach us to number our days that we may get a heart of wisdom." Psalm 90:12

Be wise about your friendships. God gifts us with many people in our lives, and each can meet different needs with their individual gifts.

But when it comes to other men, be careful. Make certain your husband gets the best of your heart and time. In our culture, a girl can "hang out" with a guy without ever seeing him in person. Women can private message a man at any part of her day or night, text him, or browse his profile.

Beware of consuming another man's time and thought that is not yours to have. Men and women have become incredibly close through social media, while the spouse is basically in the dark and has little knowledge or awareness that there is a close friendship going on with someone of the opposite sex.

This is unhealthy and dangerous, not to mention hurtful to your man. It's not wrong to be friends with another man, but keep your husband in the loop! If allowing your husband access to your social media accounts, phone, or email makes you uncomfortable, you may be crossing a line in your relationships that could hurt your marriage. Never do on a screen what you cannot do in person. Don't constantly "meet up" with a man on a screen, sharing places of your life and heart that need to be kept for your husband.

Appreciate what other friendships can offer your heart, but stay away from men who want an emotional intimacy you're uncomfortable telling your husband about. Remember, when you say *no* to the wrong thing, there is more room to say *yes* to the right things! God's heart is to bless you, not deprive you. His *no* is never deprivation, but an invitation to better things.

God, help me be honest, open, and careful with my friendships. Help me honor the spot in my heart that needs to be kept for my husband, but not expect him to be everything when You've blessed me with other wise, loving people in my life.

Dare to live above reproach in this area of social media. Dare establish and maintain healthy friendships alongside your husband rather than alone, without him. Is there anyone you need to dismiss from your life?

Day 57

"Bear one another's burdens, and so fulfill the law of
Christ." Galatians 6:2

He walks through the door, kicks off his boots, and
drops his stuff onto the floor. A kiss later, he's on the re-
cliner. And I'm buzzing around like a bee on overdrive.
The piles he's just left in the dining room leave my brain
even more crowded.

I've just spent an entire day trying to get the yard and
house away from an eternal mess. I'm nearly through, and
ready to crash—and then, he makes more mess.

Wives may yell and nag, or they could look at that tired
man with compassion. That man, who's just spent an entire day working for her and the kids.

That man, who does this five days a week whether he
feels like it or not.

That man, who provides everything from toilet paper to
vacation flights home to see your family.

The man who watches the pocketbook dwindle with
each thing a growing child needs.

The man who walks away from the roaring truck he's
wanted for so many years and keeps driving the family van
because he's saving up for a house for his wife and kids.

That man. If you appreciate *that man* verbally, you have
a good beginning place to voice your desires about his
mess. Make sure you begin with a lifestyle of appreciation!
Most times, what matters is how we view him and what
we focus on. Focus on the good and you will be able to ask
for the "bad" to change.

My husband knows that my brain hits dysfunction
when there are piles of stuff around the house for days. He
has his messy rec room/office, and he picks up most of his

mess in other parts of the house, for me. Giving and receiving will help you avoid nagging and griping!

God, help me to focus on the things he does for me rather than gripe about what he doesn't do. Help me express my desires with a foundation of appreciation.

Today, dare to appreciate first, then ask! In what ways can you bless your husband for all his hard work?

Day 58

"He has told you, O man, what is good; and what does the Lord require of you, but to do justice, and to love kindness, and to walk humbly with your God?" Micah 6:8

Loving your husband well includes letting go of your need for approval. Many women mistake agreeing with their man for having an approved place with God and their man. Sometimes, we give up the important place of wholeness for the craved place of approval in every area of life. This is idolatry.

Nothing that keeps us in a helpless grip has a good place in our hearts—even if it's a good thing. We can be dependent on good things to our own detriment when we willingly hand over God's approval for our man's approval.

Letting go of our own need for approval allows us to speak truth even when our man may want to hear something else. You can stand up for God or yourself with exemplary speech and actions. Letting go allows you to think rationally and enables you to speak constructively, or release an issue entirely.

Depending on anything for your happiness or approval renders you captive to that one thing, when in reality, God is the only one who can give you lasting joy and peace. Once you release your need for approval from another, you become free to live without it, should the need arise.

Live for the approval of God, and He will lead you to approved places with your man even if there are things on which you will never see eye-to-eye. An approved place with your man doesn't imply you both approve of all thoughts, ideas, or views the other has.

Love is always possible, always freeing, always full of truth and grace. Love releases the other from needing to comply with all thoughts and ideas in order to be loved.

God, help me release the inner need for approval, and learn to let it go. Help me be real, be myself, and be true to what You are speaking.

Today, I want us to dare hang on to truth even when our husband or friend doesn't see this truth. Dare to believe that your heart is accountable before God for receiving truth from God. In what ways can you honor your man even when you disagree with him in some area?

Day 59

"There is none good, but one; that is, God." Mark 10:18

When God brought woman to man, Adam was in awe of Eve in a holy moment of wonder over God's perfect creation. And Eve felt the same wonder over Adam.

In the garden, perfect harmony reigned. Everything around them, in them, and through them was in sync with goodness and blessing. Today, it is no longer so.

Many things around us, in us, and coming out of us are broken. One spouse will see something needing to change, and the other won't. One won't listen when they should, and continues in brokenness when there could be life. This blindness causes more brokenness.

Broken vessels no longer hold life-giving water, and before long, both spouses are dry—unless they depend individually on the Giver of Life.

He is still in sync with goodness, for God *is* good and created all good. He makes no mistakes. It remains, then, that each spouse must look to Perfection for perfect love in a world where blindness often breaks the bond between two imperfect people.

Meaning is much greater than marriage; meaning is knowing the Master. Seek to know the Master, and He will help you grow your marriage. Realize that your husband was never intended to be your all in all. Releasing an imperfect human for a Perfect God will bring you to personal, God-honoring good, and bless you with wholeness in spite of broken places.

Remember, it is God and you before it is you and your husband. God in you will draw you to your husband in freedom, because you've finally let go of *the man* and allowed the One, True God first place in your heart. Letting go of your man will, in the end, help you hang onto your man as God leads you.

Father, help me to know the Master so well that my truest meaning comes from You. Thank You that You are the only Perfect One, and in You there is complete peace.

Today, dare to release things while you get to know your Master, and do what He bids you do. How will you get very close to the heart of God today, and listen in on what to do or say?

_____
_____
_____
_____
_____
_____
_____
_____
_____
_____
_____
_____

Day 60

"And God has appointed in the church first apostles, second prophets, third teachers, then miracles, then gifts of healing, helping, administrating, and various kinds of tongues." 1 Corinthians 12:28

Mothers and wives are often credited for being on call 24/7. The world seems to know how many diapers we have to buy and how frustrating it is when the juice spills one more time. But not enough of the world pays attention to fathers and the load they carry.

Some people say that even though men think less about household chores or needs, on average they think more about financial concerns. They add that only 25 percent of them get enough sleep, while 33 percent of women get enough. One-hundred-fifty hours of interviews with fathers from various walks of life lets us know how many men feel stretched thin. On a scale of one to ten, all of them except two gave a ten. Those two men gave an eight.

This lifestyle of feeling stretched thin often leads to depression.

Many fathers work long hours, are there for each child, and think about their wives. They get little time to relax unless they just take it.

Many women seem to think that men should turn into a domestic servant as soon as his label of boss, coworker, or employee gets peeled off each evening. Though there are viable times where women need their husbands' help, we often forget that our man may have had a day on the run and desperately needs some time alone before engaging with his entire family. Or we forget that he needs a hunting trip simply for relaxation just as she needs that shopping trip with her mom and sisters.

A happy marriage includes giving each other rejuvenation times when they are needed most. Ask for yours, and make certain you give him his. If he seems depressed or listless, perhaps there's a need you can notice and encourage him to fill?

God, forgive me for not realizing how much my man needs a break. Help me to give him time with his friends just as I go out with mine.

If your man enjoys time out, today's dare includes heading his way with a smile and an offer to give him the weekend for his own rest and rejuvenation. How will you give him time this week?

_____

_____

_____

_____

_____

_____

_____

_____

_____

Day 61

"Then the Lord God said, 'It is not good that man should be alone; I will make him a helper fit for him.'" Genesis 2:18

Ladies, we get to be confident because *we were created.* Creation doesn't get to pronounce on itself a different name than the one given by the Creator. Neither does it get to change itself without some undesired repercussions.

Some women may be called to a leadership position, or a job may open for her that she and her husband both desire her to take. Still, she is created by God with unique qualities to bring to the relationship. Embracing womanhood doesn't mean we all do the same thing; we simply live out our gifts as women without trying to prove ourselves in areas we aren't as good at.

One survey shows that even when both spouses work, the average man still puts in more hours at work while the average woman puts in more hours of housework. Let feminists cry as long and hard as they desire; they will never be able to undo the work of a good Creator God who designed each of His creation to do what it does best for the good of the entire universe.

Rather than fight who we naturally are, why not build up, grow, and become even better at what we do? Don't doctors and lawyers do that, and aren't we glad the lawyer isn't trying to come alongside the doctor in some complicated heart surgery to prove that he's equally capable?

If he did, the lawyer would not prove his own worth any more than if he went to the courtroom and did his job as best he could. See this, ladies, we are not to prove anything—we are to be everything we already are.

The doctor will have his mind cluttered and his hands less focused if there's a lawyer at his side, insisting to "help." Likewise, your man will be more frustrated and less efficient if you are not allowing him to be the man while you joyfully live your role as woman.

All of nature has a place. All was created for its own purpose. In marriage, even more so! Love your man well by loving God's creation in both of you.

Father, forgive us for trying to prove that we are equally capable in things You've designed men to do best, then shrink back when the hardest, scariest, dirtiest jobs are available.

In today's dare, we will fully embrace that we are created differently from men. Rather than proving ourselves, we will grow ourselves. How will you bless your husband rather than try to prove yourself to him?

_____

_____

_____

_____

_____

_____

_____

_____

Day 62

"An excellent wife is a crown to her husband." Proverbs 12:4

Love your man well by doing your life well, even housework and daily chores. Do those things well, and *the work will change from being something you resent to something you channel love through.* It will be part of your beauty.

Cultivate the beauty in you and around you—and the world will be better because you are there. Even cleaning a bathroom is a means of bringing beauty into your man's world. What would happen if no one cleaned it? I smile when I'm scrubbing a toilet and realize there's actually a lot of meaning in what I'm doing!

Every woman has beauty to cultivate. Most of us are not Hollywood Stars, but we have natural beauty to care for and bring alive—beauty of body, soul, and spirit. What an honor to bring beauty into the world!

God is the Creator of beauty. Breathtaking sunrises, mountain summits, eye-catching flowers, shimmering waters—but most men will say that a woman's beauty crowns them all. He desires her more than the mountaintop or sun setting over the water. And he desires her inner beauty as much as, or more than, her outer beauty.

If women only knew that it is the entirety of their beauty that captivates a man's heart, women would work on their spirit as much as they face the mirror.

A beautiful spirit is a serving spirit. Women were designed by God to nurture, and our man needs this side of us. Clean that bathroom, wash those dishes, cook that meal with a thankful heart, knowing that mundane chores lead you to monumental love.

Love your man well by bringing beauty of body, soul, and spirit to his life. Clean the toilets with a thankful heart by realizing that even the worst chore in the house brings beauty to the house he lives in. Ask him for help when you need it, but find meaning in menial tasks as well as ones you enjoy more!

Father, help me not to resent the things I do well, but to realize they are a means of bringing beauty into our world.

Dare view even the most menial tasks as a way to bring beauty to the world. Create an atmosphere of rest and peace because of your God-given nature to bring beauty to everything around you. How will you help to create a peaceful home environment that you and your husband can enjoy together?

_____

_____

_____

_____

_____

_____

_____

_____

Day 63

"Therefore a man shall leave his father and his mother and hold fast to his wife, and they shall become one flesh." Genesis 2:24

I can't wait to make omelets for my husband this morning. No, I'm not being facetious, nor am I that 1930s housewife who pretends to like serving my husband because that's what society expects of me.

I know what it's like to perform for love, and now, I know what it's like to serve in love.

I know all about trying to please so I can have the pleasure of someone being pleased with me, and now I'm discovering what it's like to create a pleasing atmosphere based on the fruits of the Spirit.

Performing for love is very different from being filled with love. Many women mistake shedding codependency for selfishness and lack of care for others. When we live in the Spirit, we learn to stand on our own two feet while still serving with our own two hands.

The fruit of the spirit is love. Love gives, serves, cares about, and nurtures another. Love is not selfish, vain, self-absorbed, or impatient. Love is best seen by the atmosphere it creates.

Performing for love is exhausting, because you never feel like you've given enough. You are never able to say *no*.

Serving because you are loved means you are not serving *for* love—you are serving because you *are* loved, and you're in love with Jesus, and He is love. You live like He did, because you're filled with Himself. You know your limitations, just as the Son of God did when he crossed over to the other side of the lake to rest, away from the crowds.

From this place of knowing how loved you are, you are able to love well, give unselfishly, and know your limitations simultaneously. Performance gives way to peace, and you find joy in serving from a place of rest. When the weekend rolls around, you may actually enjoy scrubbing those toilets or cooking up a special breakfast!

Love your husband well by serving because you love him, rather than performing just so you can be loved.

Father, forgive me for performing for love when all You want is for me to know Your love and live out of that love.

Today, dare to walk unselfishly, not because you need to gain anything, but because Christ in you has much to give. How will you love on your husband today?

_____

_____

_____

_____

_____

_____

_____

_____

Day 64

"The reward for humility and fear of the Lord is riches and honor and life." Proverbs 22:4

Your man needs you to love him by deferring to him when the need arises.

If you're bristling here, remember that deferring is something every mature person knows how to do.

Mari's husband had purchased a home in need of repair, and together they spent many thousands of dollars to fix it up. Months later when the money was dry, her man wanted to pave the long driveway with gravel for an upcoming party being held there.

Mari didn't think it was necessary; she may have been absolutely right. She was smart, analytical, and level-headed, with a lot of wisdom in many areas. The driveway would have been workable for the upcoming night, but her man wanted things to look good, not just be serviceable.

Mari had a choice—she could keep insisting and turn the conflicting thoughts into a conflicted marriage. But she knew what she needed to do—honestly speak her mind, give her reasons, then back off if her man decided to keep his plan. Mari was smart in more ways than one and decided on the latter. Her bank account may suffer, but her home and marriage will thrive.

Love your man well by deferring to his leadership after you've spoken your mind!

Father, help me speak my mind, then defer to my man. Help me keep Your peace more than keep my plans.

Today, the dare is to believe there is greater blessing in following God's plan for leadership than in insisting on your own way. In what area is God asking you to defer to your husband?

Day 65

"How long will scoffers delight in their scoffing and fools hate knowledge?" Proverbs 1:22

The girls argued heatedly the other day, interrupting and rudely demanding the other see her side of things.

My husband came on the scene and began intervening. "Girls, you're not listening, you're interrupting. You're not trying to understand, you're trying to be understood."

The heat in the room came down ten degrees, instantly. "Listen to gain understanding," he encouraged.

Men and women often perceive things differently. If a man comes home with a marriage book, his wife will likely feel loved and appreciate that he cares about their relationship. But if a wife brings one home, he will likely feel threatened and wish to avoid what could mean more hours of discussion. Neither one of their feelings is *wrong*–they simply need to understand and bridge the gap with loving communication.

A husband can see the book and realize his wife simply wants her relationship with him to grow. She wants answers so they can be better, together. And a wife, when her husband ignores the book she brought home, can begin building him up rather than feel like he doesn't care about his relationship with her. Both have needs; both see the answer to those needs in entirely different ways.

A happy marriage is a listening marriage. Intimacy means you are both entirely honest and are both able to feel heard and understood whether or not you think alike.

Father, help us both to be heard in a safe place.
Help me give this to my man, and to ask it from him.

Today, dare listen in order to gain understanding. Dare ask your man for the same consideration, and refuse to argue. How will you conduct yourself in the next difficult conversation?

Day 66

"I adjure you, O daughters of Jerusalem,
if you find my beloved, that you tell him I am sick
with love." The Song of Solomon 5:8

If your man is like most, one of his greatest desires is that you enjoy the gift of sex. Though you rise to the occasion to meet his biological need for sex, you are also a sexual being with needs of your own—and *he wants to know he is satisfying you.*

A good man will want to share the joy of sex with you as much as he wants to be satisfied by it. Sex is intended for mutual pleasure and a deep, satisfying heart connection.

Loving your man well includes letting him know what you need even as you rise to meet his need. Working to get to mutual pleasure is a gift to him and will bring him much joy in the end. Don't be afraid to ask for it; don't cease your quest for it.

Gifts are received with joy. Are you receiving this gift and making much of it? Your man needs this from you—and you need it for yourself even more than you know! We are sexual beings, designed to need sexual release as well as the accompanying connection to our man.

Pursuing your own fulfillment rather than resigning yourself to a life void of sexual pleasure is one of the greatest gifts you can give your husband. He wants to connect with *you,* a person engaged. He wants the emotional connection as well as the physical release, and this is best realized when you are able to enjoy it with abandon!

Take note of anything hindering your joy, whether it be an emotional, physical, or spiritual matter. Care for the negative things so that you can enjoy the good things! Make it a matter to pursue rather than one you ignore. If your husband is uncaring or selfish, appeal to him in these areas rather than resign yourself to living without.

Father, help me receive this great gift with joy, and make it one of the top priorities in our relationship.

Today, dare pursue your man and initiate sex. Perhaps take a dare to try something new! What step will you take to improve or continue your sexual intimacy?

Day 67

"But I say to you that everyone who looks at a woman with lustful intent has already committed adultery with her in his heart. If your right eye causes you to sin, tear it out and put it away." Matthew 5:28&29a

Your man needs you to love him by safeguarding your intimacy, both with your own integrity and with his. Immersing yourself in erotic novels or indulging in sexual movies can lead you to dissatisfaction with your husband just as pornography can lead him away from you.

Your heart needs to be in a place of acceptance and love toward a very real human man rather than fantasizing about men you read about or see. This becomes difficult when you're constantly engaged with the abnormal— and before long, a spot that should be his becomes theirs. Guard your heart!

Your husband needs you to stand against pornography in the same way you stand against an affair. Porn is a screen affair rather than a physical one—and both will eat away your connection to each other.

Many Christian men are subject to this vice while their wives remain in a place of emotional distress. And I'm increasingly aware that many women and girls fall prey to the same. You have a right—and duty—to shun this vice and refuse to allow its entrance or presence in your home.

In dire situations where men don't respond with repentance and change, women are often judged more for leaving than men are for their lack of cleaving. If he doesn't respond with repentance and change, consider not responding to his sexual advances. He needs to know this is where you are at more than he needs you to coddle him where he is at.

A real man knows women are not objects to be devoured whenever he wants, but sex is a gift from the woman he wanted and chose. And real women know that romance is to be enjoyed with the real man she chose and married rather than fantasized about with men in books and movies.

Your marriage bed is sacred, intimate between you and him alone. Your feelings of betrayal are there because when a man brings other women to the screen, he brings them to the bed (spiritually speaking). And remember, if you are a woman falling to the same prey, you are also being unfaithful.

Neither of you should stay silent while the other keeps indulging. If this is you, sister, know that there are answers for every case that will lead you to wholeness. Take courage, and stand strong.

Lord, keep my man free from this vice, and help me stand for the purity of our marriage.

Dare take a strong stand, in love, against this vice that will keep you from true love with each other. How will you stand for purity and love in your sexual relationship?

Day 68

"Well done, good and faithful servant.
You have been faithful over a little; I will set you over
much." Matthew 25:23a

Your man needs you to love him well by not burying your talents. Did you know that you can be stronger than he, but still honor his strength? You can make more money than he does, but still appreciate what he provides for you and the kids. You can be smarter than he is, but never put him down—and rather, lift him up. You can be more analytical, but never make him feel stupid.

Some driven women are married to men who are more laid back, meditative, thoughtful, and calm. They easily spin circles around their husbands and sometimes feel quite competent without them.

Loving your man means that you retain your own gifts without faulting him for not having the same. Whether you are more often "right" or have the "best" idea, you simply learn to grow his manhood by appreciating all of his own gifts and never putting him down. Don't make him feel like he should run in the same circles you do, accomplishing just as much and thinking just as analytically.

Honor him, boost him; create a safe environment for him while you keep enjoying your own God-given talents! Realize he's filling an entirely different role or spot in the universe, and show him great honor by noticing and admiring his place.

Lord, help me not to bury my talents in a false pretense of honor. Help me honor my husband for his own gifts and never demean him or make him feel low in my presence.

Pause today and consider what the world would be like if everyone was just like you. Then, go to your husband with a sincere compliment on something he's done. How will you show appreciation for his contribution to the world?

_____
_____
_____
_____
_____
_____
_____
_____
_____
_____
_____
_____
_____
_____
_____
_____
_____
_____

Day 69

"So the Lord God caused a deep sleep to fall upon the man, and while he slept took one of his ribs and closed up its place with flesh. And the rib that the Lord God had taken from the man he made into a woman and brought her to the man. Then the man said, 'This at last is bone of my bones and flesh of my flesh.'" Genesis 2:21-23a

He winked at me across the gym, and I winked back. My husband and I are *friends*. We are far from perfect and have many things to learn, but friendship is important to us.

Loneliness is one of the greatest enemies in marriage. Sometimes, a couple's focus on leadership and submission leads them to compartmentalize each other to the point of losing out on the fun and enjoyment they can have living life together. They become more focused on who's in charge and who should follow than on loving each other well. This is a great loss.

Learn to live as best friends. Best friends share ideas and thoughts while giving mutual respect toward each other. Best friends know not to criticize each other in public. Best friends know to give and take. Often, they even know how to let the other win, and how to give in.

When the Christian church preaches leadership, they often lose out on friendship. I've seen many, many women living with quiet grief and inner burdens, but no voice to share them well—*and no man to hear her heart well.* Know that you both need the same things best friends need—and a woman who is fully alive and free has a lot more to offer than a burdened, silent one.

When a woman wants face-to-face contact and communication while a man may want space, friendship reaches out to bridge the gap. Friends both have needs and they both give and receive. A woman can learn to give space while a man learns to talk more—or at least, to listen to her talk!

When you live as friends, you are better able to follow his lead when he needs you to do so. If there are things you can't reach conclusion about, remember the Lord calls you to honor his leadership, and defer to Him. If you live as friends, deferring to His leadership won't be all that difficult!

God, I want to be my husband's best friend. Please remove any selfishness or wrong ideas of what leadership is, so that we can enjoy the blessings of friendship.

Dare to pursue a friendship in marriage, and to let your man know if he is squelching you. How will you take the dare to come fully alive while maintaining love and respect toward your husband?

Day 70

"Because your steadfast love is better than life, my lips will praise you. So I will bless you as long as I live; in your name I will lift up my hands. My soul will be satisfied as with fat and rich food, and my mouth will praise you with joyful lips." Psalm 63:3–5

In my codependent state, I remember carrying a distinct burden that it was my job to keep my husband happy. I'd seen other marriages struggle when the wife was no longer "happy enough" or "serving enough." I determined not to ruin my marriage; I would be everything I thought it would take to make my husband happy and keep his heart.

In an effort to keep his heart, I hid my own. And I struggled to survive.

The result in my marriage wasn't what I was looking for. No real man wants a woman walking after him, needless and obliging, in a vain effort to please him. When I broke free, I felt fully human, fully alive, and fully free.

More than trying to be everything you think your man wants you to be (and if your husband is selfish, he may actually want you as his puppet), you need to gift him with who God has created you to be.

Though you are a joy-giver, you are not responsible for his joy.

Though you are a kind person who loves to bless him, it is not your duty to be everything for him.

Though you bring wellness to him, you are not responsible for his well-being.

Though you serve him well, you are not his servant.

God created each of us to be responsible for ourselves. You cannot look to your man for filling each spot in your heart, just as he cannot look to you for each spot in his.

Trying to be everything to each other leads to more anger and depression rather than more love and joy.

Don't try to prove anything—just be entirely full of Proven Love. Proven Love will grace you with wellness; performance will drag you to weakness. You cannot stay healthy and rejuvenated when you are drained from taking full responsibility for his heart. Loving your man well means you release yourself from being fully responsible for your man.

When you learn this, you will serve him even better—though you also learn your limitations. You will serve him with joy. You will give often, and give well. "God loves a *cheerful* giver (2 Corinthians 9:7). Cheerfulness comes with the freedom of love, not the burden of false responsibility.

Father, help me to love my husband with deep, unselfish, Proven Love—but realize I have nothing to prove.

Today, dare give lavish amounts of joy, love, and kindness while realizing that the burden of his well-being is not ultimately on you. How will you continue to serve him without taking full responsibility for his everything?

Day 71

"If we confess our sins, he is faithful and just to forgive us our sins and to cleanse us from all unrighteousness." 1 John 1:9

Your man needs you to release him.

Have you ever heard that men compartmentalize their lives, while a woman's mind has everything going on at once? In the case of failure and forgiveness, nothing could be more true.

It may be that your man is able to mess up greatly one day, repent the next day, and move on. You may have a difficult time releasing things and moving on; his failure becomes the looming object in your heart and you are devastated months (or years) later.

Though you need your man to care for your heart and put forth great effort to heal what he's broken, he also needs you to extend your heart of forgiveness before you feel ready to do so. If he's repented and you keep holding on, you can destroy his own trust toward you. Your man needs to know that you are able to release.

Forgiveness doesn't imply trust or approval; it simply releases him from having to pay for what he's done.

Trust must be earned. You will drive yourself into the ground if you berate yourself for not being able to trust before he has proved himself with repentance and change over a period of time.

If he has not clearly repented, however, and you remain in doubt as to his heart, you may need to care for your heart by getting others involved. Loving your husband well simply means that you live fairly. Sometimes, you need to extend your forgiveness before he regains your trust, because, though forgiveness can be granted quickly, trust needs to be earned over a period of time.

Because he is as human as you are, he will fail you as you fail him. When you are certain that he has moved on in repentance, release him, and follow him to freedom. Though your heart is still wounded, don't assume his heart is still in sin. Know the difference between forgiveness and trust, keep walking, and God will bring you through to a better place.

Father, help me not to hold grudges, but forgive quickly just as I want him to forgive me.

Today, dare believe that you can extend forgiveness before you are able to trust. In what ways will you express forgiveness to your husband even when, for some of you, trusting fully may be impossible?

_____

_____

_____

_____

_____

_____

_____

Day 72

"He who dwells in the shelter of the Most High will abide in the shadow of the Almighty. I will say to the Lord, 'My refuge and my fortress, my God, in whom I trust.' For he will deliver you from the snare of the fowler and from the deadly pestilence." Psalm 91:1–3

Your man needs to know he is safe to share his feelings with you.

He may need to learn that it's OK to have emotions and feelings. You may be certain he has them, though you may not know how he processes them—or if he even does.

If life is full of unpleasant ripples, you may be certain there are many bottled feelings he doesn't know what to do with. Give him a safe place to speak. Ask him questions. Ask for his thoughts on matters of the heart. You need never tiptoe around your man, trying to keep him happy, but you do need to give him a safe place to process.

When men don't have a safe place to process, they often do one of two things. They may avoid you, or take it out on you. Because you are the closest one to him, you will take the brunt of it either way, not because his issues are necessarily your fault, but because you are there.

He only needs to know that you truly care about his heart, and he can safely let you know what is going on. Even if he messes up in *how he lets you know,* you can listen in to let him know that it's okay *to let you know.* You can also ask him to share his heart in gentle ways that are easier for you to hear and respond to.

When you release your need for his approval, you can hear his disapproval of you without crumbling and taking personal offense. Receive all truth and allow it to work good in your life by realizing that no person sees and knows their blind spots at all times—including yourself. Love him well by listening well!

God, forgive me for being so self-absorbed that I cannot handle the difficult aspects of my husband's heart. Help me be a safe place for him to process.

Dare to work toward a relationship with your man where there is nothing to bottle up out of fear that you will blow it up. Be a safe place, not only for the good, but the negative things of his heart. How will you be strong enough to hear all of his heart?

Day 73

"Do not be anxious about anything, but in everything by prayer and supplication with thanksgiving let your requests be made known to God." Philippians 4:6

"I had a girlfriend once," he said, "and she wouldn't stop talking. We could start at eight and not be done til midnight. I moved on, and I'm so glad I did. My wife and I don't always agree, but she's a hundred times better than any other girl I've dated."

I loved his wife. She wasn't super emotional and lived in an easygoing manner. I could picture her disagreeing with her husband while not creating a mountain out of a molehill. She was able to relax rather than rush.

I, on the other hand, needed to learn to let go. I grew up in a family of seven girls who talked, talked, and talked some more about everything on our hearts and minds. We were a pack. We walked into one another's rooms without knocking and snooped through one another's purses, journals, and phones. When we felt something, we discussed it—always, intensely, together. Knowing everything about one another was proof of our love for one another.

This kind of approach often doesn't work so well in our marriages. I learned to wait for better times to talk, and I learned that it was OK if we couldn't talk everything through. There are some basics that must be talked through or your marriage will crumble—but not everything difficult needs to get attention each day until it is cared for.

Men often move on quickly after disagreeing with each other. They may or may not confront the disagreement, and if they do, it is probably short and to the point—then *over*. Even an apology is given quickly, perhaps with no eye contact to each other. Then, they *move on*.

Give your man more breathing time than you ask for discussion time over things you don't agree with. Learn to love in the middle of unresolved topics when you know that you have solid ground on the vital ones. Then, work toward a healthy balance of communication where you are not squelched or pent up, but have an ear for the things you need.

Father, help me learn to give time and space for the positive even when there is more negative to resolve in its own time.

Today, dare to let go before the issue is gone. Dare love positively even when something negative needs attention. In what ways will you show patience and love before an issue is resolved?

_____

_____

_____

_____

_____

_____

_____

Day 74

"If my people who are called by my name humble themselves, and pray and seek my face and turn from their wicked ways, then I will hear from heaven and will forgive their sin and heal their land." 2 Chronicles 7:14

Her jaw dropped, and her mind spun. How could he? His defense went up. How could she?

Hitting an impasse where something is viewed in polar opposite ways is not pleasant, but it happens. Disagreeing happens in the best and worst marriages because we are both human with less-than-perfect perspectives on life.

Her mind clouded over until she was willing to repent and ask forgiveness for her part. It didn't matter if she was right or wrong in what she wanted him to see—what mattered was that she had failed and needed to ask for forgiveness.

She sat on the bed and swallowed hard. What if he thought he was justified and she the only one wrong? What if? But *peace with Christ was of greater importance than justification with her husband*, so she spoke the words.

"I'm sorry." There, it was out.

She wanted peace more than she wanted an apology from her man. And as the days progressed, heaven came down, and she was filled with an awareness of Christ and love such as she had rarely experienced before.

The trouble was still there. Nothing had been resolved. But what had made her want to crack a few days before no longer ate her up. See this—we are not responsible for solving *everything*, but when we fail, we are responsible to repent of *something*.

When you refuse to live in your own sin regardless of someone else's failure, you can't be eaten up; you can only be lifted up. Loving your man well means you understand that he dies for honor easier than he apologizes to a woman he feels disrespected by. Though this is no excuse for him not to apologize, it does motivate us to honor him in conflict and apologize when we disrespect him. If he is called to do what is unnatural to him, so are we!

Lord, forgive us for failing our men more often than we apologize to our men. Forgive us for not taking initiative quickly even when he has also failed.

Today's dare urges you to go to your man with an apology whether or not he has offered his own. Dare to live with a cloudless heart! How will you keep your own heaven clear?

_____

_____

_____

_____

_____

_____

_____

Day 75

"However, let each one of you love his wife as himself,
and let the wife see that she respects her husband."
Ephesians 5:33

If couples learned how to decode each other rather than react to each other, divorce attorneys would soon be out of business.

In today's culture, a woman needing unconditional love is smiled upon while a man needing unconditional respect is called sexist. We've become a love-dominated culture, void of understanding that most men (according to some surveys, up to 74 percent, or more) would rather feel alone and unloved than feel inadequate and disrespected.

This is not prideful; it is purposeful. God knows what He's doing when He wires us differently.

And your need to be loved, sister, is not weak; it is wonderful. God knew what He was doing when He created you.

When we fail to respect a man, we emasculate him without knowing what we're doing. He will be devastated if you don't respect him just as you are devastated if he doesn't love you.

Few women are married to evil beasts who want to make them feel unloved. Men simply think differently. When there's conflict, a woman will usually feel unloved and a man will feel disrespected. Imagine if, rather than react, he looked at her and said, "I feel disrespected by what you said; did you feel unloved by something I said?" And if you, rather than react when you feel unloved, are able to express, "I feel unloved by you; do you feel disrespected by me?"

When a man feels disrespected, he often reacts unlovingly, and when a woman feels unloved, it is very difficult to show respect. Decoding each other's negative reactions rather than creating even more puts an end to the cycle.

Which one will change first? I dare say the one who is most mature!

Father, help my husband and me learn to decode each other rather than devastate each other even further. Forgive us for our lack of wisdom.

Today's dare is to look at your man the next time he makes you feel unloved and to say, "I feel unloved by what you just said—are you also feeling disrespected by what I did or said?" How will you decode his actions rather than destroy his heart?

Day 76

"Give, and it will be given to you. Good measure, pressed down, shaken together, running over, will be put into your lap. For with the measure you use it will be measured back to you." Luke 6:38

I've heard women ask, "What shall I do when my husband seems oblivious to my emotional needs, then wants me sexually at night? Sometimes I sob my heart out after sex because I feel used."

And I've read of a wife who moved to another bedroom because, she said, "He wasn't meeting my emotional needs. He doesn't know when he's not meeting them, really. But I'm standing up for myself."

Not every wife is married to a man who makes sure everything is good relationally before they engage sexually. Women ask, "What shall I do? He doesn't get it."

Dear wife, is your man faithful to you? Does he love you? If you can answer those two questions with a yes, you may rest assured there is blessing in giving him your sexual love in spite of emotional odds in your heart.

If we desire more time, more communication, more consideration, more of this or that, we may freely give and enjoy sex even when other areas of our relationship are lacking. (Of course, there are levels of hurt and abuse other than unfaithfulness that warrant refusal of sex; I'm speaking here of less-than-drastic needs.)

Not every wife has a faithful man, and those who don't would give much for a man who walks out his love in committed faithfulness even while he lacks in other areas. If your man truly loves you, love him back with sexual intimacy. (That said, if you have debilitating emotional pain, of course there are times to take a sexual break so you can work things out. Choose wisely when or if to do so, then strive to find answers so you can come together again quickly.)

Because sex binds our souls as well as our bodies, you can see it as one way to be emotionally connected rather than withhold it because you feel a lack of connection. Keep working toward having your heart needs met while you hold onto the gift of sex!

Father, help me see sex as one of many ways to build emotional connection rather than refuse sex because I lack emotional fulfillment.

Dare to engage in sex with your man even when there are unmet needs elsewhere—unless, of course, those needs are major and you need time off to repair a broken heart. What truths can you agree with to help you see the blessing in sexual love?

_____

_____

_____

_____

_____

_____

Day 77

"I praise you, for I am fearfully and wonderfully made. Wonderful are your works; my soul knows it very well."
Psalm 149:14

Women are incredibly attracted to the strength of a man, whether it be the strength of love, character, purpose, service, or provision and care. The strength of his arms, voice, or any other physical quality is incredibly appealing and draws us in with a force we cannot explain. Every woman wants to see her man strong.

We do not always realize the power we have in making our man want to be strong.

When he first laid eyes on you and got to know you, it was your personal characteristics, beauty, and femininity that drew out his best manly characteristics. Just you being you made him want to be strong and provide. You literally beckoned to his heart without even trying.

Loving our husband well means remembering the girl we were when he was first drawn to us. It means not shedding the grace, kindness, and femininity just because we are older and have been married for many years. In short, it means *don't take him for granted, and keep right on beckoning to his manhood.*

Learn to beckon to his natural desires to care for you rather than badger him into being something no man was meant to be. Learn about who he was created to be, and allow your own created self to appeal to his heart by staying kind, loving, and honoring. When you walk in who God created you to be, you allow the natural, God-given instincts a chance to come alive rather than want to turn off.

Refuse to join the crowd of women who take their men for granted. Choose, instead, to be the girl he fell in love with! Though you are not responsible for his actions toward you, you can fan his flame or dull it. Which will you choose, today?

Father, help me keep characteristics that make it easy for my man to be drawn to. Help me not give up the graces that attract him, and help me never take him for granted.

Today's dare means we ponder who we were as the girl he dated and fell in love with, then ask ourselves who we are, now. Dare put away any snarky attitudes or unbecoming habits that disgrace your womanhood. What habits can you put away today, and what will you replace them with?

Day 78

"And let us consider how to stir up one another
to love and good works . . . encouraging one another."
Hebrews 10:24&25

God must have laughed when He gave me a man who's chiefest love languages include words of affirmation. Me, the former Amish girl who was raised with people denying praise rather than dishing up raves.

I'm the girl who needed to learn that it really wasn't proud to say *thank you* when someone verbalized something good and admirable in me. I grew up in a quiet world void of social media while the rest of the world posted all things wonderful *about themselves* to the world. While other girls posted beautiful selfies almost daily, I did everything possible *not to be too beautiful.*

It took a while to learn that my man's need for affirming words from his wife isn't *prideful*—and he needs it as much as I need quality time together. Just because I don't need many words doesn't mean I can't give words.

I pass him by today, and lightly touch his rock-solid abs. I can simply notice them, or I can actually *mention* them. "Your abs look amazing!" I comment. He thanks me, and I move on. A little comment takes very little time or effort while it works the right chord in my husband's heart.

Speaking your man's love language may mean stepping outside your own needs and doing something on purpose that feels out of line with your natural tendencies. But how hard is it, *really*, to do the little things? Learn what his needs are, and do your best to meet them!

Father, help me reach out and fill those areas of my husband's life so he won't be lacking the things that make him come alive.

Today, dare to ask your man what makes his heart feel most loved in your relationship. Then, dare to do it even before you understand it! How will you find out and fill his specific love language?

_____

_____

_____

_____

_____

_____

_____

_____

_____

_____

_____

_____

_____

_____

_____

_____

Day 79

"Two are better than one, because they have a good reward for their toil. For if they fall, one will lift up his fellow. But woe to him who is alone when he falls and has not another to lift him up! Again, if two lie together, they keep warm, but how can one keep warm alone? And though a man might prevail against one who is alone, two will withstand him—a threefold cord is not quickly broken." Ecclesiastes 4:9–12

I watched my friend splash and play in the water, but more than that, I saw her smile. She loved spending time with her husband.

She laughed when he dived into the water; she came close for a touch. All afternoon, there was rest and peace about her spirit, and when he spoke of a subject she didn't agree with, she mentioned it respectfully without a trace of bitterness.

She had two kids, a boy and a girl, but she wasn't one of those mamas who dotes on the kids every minute while ignoring her man. *He got part of her, too.* Some of her thought, her joy, her life was directed his way on that sunny summer day as we all swam in the deep blue. And he was satisfied.

It's becoming rather easy to note when a man seems satisfied and joyful with his wife, because it's so rare. But when a woman becomes her man's friend, his cup is full. He married her because he wanted a friend more than he wanted a mother for his kids, a cook, or someone to direct his life.

He wanted a woman to share life with, and sharing life is more than sharing a bed—it is sharing smiles and thoughts and cares and touch. It is looking his way even when you don't have to.

Einai is the Greek word used in Titus 2:4–5 where it says the young women are to love their husbands. "And so train the young women to love their husbands and children, to be self controlled, pure, working at home, kind, submissive to their own husbands, that the word of God may not be reviled."

Two of the definitions for *Einai* are "to lust after" and "to please well." This includes, but is more than, sex. A good man wants all of you, not just your body. He craves your smiles, care, touch, and joy more than you know, and even a quiet man notices when those things seem directed to everyone but himself.

Notice that it says, "to love their husbands" before it says, "to love their children." If we get this one right, loving our man well becomes one of the greatest gifts we give our children.

Father, help me give more of my time, joy, and energy to my man, knowing that the kids gain more from watching me enjoy their father than they do from having all my time.

Today, dare *not* to spend extra time with your kids if that's what it takes to get some time in with your man. What will you do to actively pursue your husband?

Day 80

"If a kingdom is divided against itself, that kingdom cannot stand. And if a house is divided against itself, that house will not be able to stand." Mark 3:24–25

I remember the morning I texted my husband a love text just as he woke, though I'd been up for a while. He came into the kitchen and greeted me with a grin and a gentle kiss.

The table was full of watching kids, and our oldest daughter remarked, "I love that you and daddy have been married for so long, and you're still romantic!"

I smiled and pulled away. "Marriage is no fun unless it's romantic," I replied. "Daddy is more than just my roommate!"

Our husband is not just the provider, the bread winner, the taxi. He is to be our friend. He is to be a joy and delight to us. We are to love him with more than agape love; we are to love him with romantic love.

If there is a block in your heart to this kind of love, find out why. If you can't get to the bottom of it on your own, reach out for help and learn what in him or yourself makes you shy away rather than come close. Do whatever it takes to refuse a cold, distant marriage, and you will bless your man with a warm, close friendship.

Do it if the problem is you; do it even if the problem is him. More than likely, it is both of you. Be more afraid of not finding answers than you are of not living love. Be less willing to become brittle than you are to become vulnerable.

Father, help me believe that we can be romantic
once again, and help me to do what it takes to get there
even if it will be a long, painful process.

Today, dare to be romantic! If that seems impossible, begin your journey of finding out why. Dare refuse a life of dissatisfaction; reach out for answers. What will you do to remove whatever is blocking the romance in your marriage?

Day 81

"Know this, my beloved [sisters]: let every person be
quick to hear." James 1:19a

"Could you at least listen, and express understanding
even when you don't agree?" he asked me.

We were in one of those *I want to be understood* conversations. I wasn't doing so well at the whole reflective
listening thing because I wanted more than anything for
him to listen well to *me*. After all, I was internally assured
that I had the best idea and the wisest thought and I knew
how to get things rolling fluidly for the benefit of the entire
family.

But he didn't think so. And we both "knew" the other
wasn't as wise as we both "knew" we were.

Reflective listening means you listen so well that at the
end of a conversation it is possible for someone to feel understood and respected, even if you still don't agree. You
lean in, hear what they feel, listen to their body language
as well as their words, and put yourself in their shoes.
(Don't worry, you don't have to walk in their shoes—you
just need to wear them for a minute.)

I took the request seriously because I want that from
him—and I know what it feels like to want it even more
than I want anything to change. Like my friend, who told
me, "My husband is hearing me for the first time and it
takes the issue at hand to a much lower level. I realize that
I mostly wanted to feel loved and I wanted to know he
heard my heart."

Her man was smart and went to counseling to learn
how to nurture his wife's heart because he knew it was
breaking. He saw what he never saw before—how to make
his wife feel heard—and he learned how to listen well. Can

we do the same for our men? Can we listen and honor them so well that they feel heard whether or not we agree?

Love your man well by learning the art of reflective listening!

Lord, help me to listen in on what my husband does, feels, says, and thinks so well that he feels heard and respected even when I disagree.

Dare try something new in your next conversation. Focus more on rightly listening than on being right! How will you reflect his words back to him in order to understand him fully?

_____

_____

_____

_____

_____

_____

_____

_____

_____

Day 82

"For we are his workmanship, created in Christ Jesus for good works, which God prepared beforehand, that we should walk in them." Ephesians 2:10

My husband and I went out for dinner one night some years back, and though I was grateful for his time and attention, I couldn't help but wonder why most married men often don't feel the same need for quality time as women do.

If, in the dating years, they arrive eagerly on a girl's doorstep with flowers in hand and leave reluctantly many hours later, why, years later, are they often occupied in other goals and share much less time together?

That night I asked my husband the daunting question. His reply was forthright and simple. "It's because that was the only time we had to spend together; now we get to *live together*."

Simple, is it not? Once more, a light bulb went on in my head.

Loving well means we learn to release well. We live well by pursuing our own things on the side rather than expecting him to constantly be at our side.

Learn to enjoy your own hobbies and friends while you release your man to his. A healthy marriage often has both spouses doing a few separate things for rejuvenation, then coming back together, refreshed. Two refreshed people coming together create a happier marriage than two stressed people who are both on a tight line of trying to keep each other happy.

Allow your man some time on his own, and hang out with your friends—or even your kids! Throw a blanket on the floor and place your largest bowl of popcorn in the middle while you talk with your kids, read to them, snuggle with them. Avoid self-pity at all costs.

There are few things as unattractive as a girl who pities herself at every turn, or a girl who wallows in self-pity instead of clearly (and gently) communicating her needs. Pursue time with your man, but allow him to have time away, as well.

Quality time is of more importance than great quantities of time! Releasing your man will almost certainly bring you time of greater quality even if you let go of quantity.

Father, help me release my husband from the burden of being everything for me. Help me pursue the good and beautiful so I have my own life to invite him into rather than expecting him to be my life.

If you've been expecting your man to be your all in all, take a dare and pursue something on your own that will make you happy and delightful. How will you release your man to have his own time?

_____

_____

_____

_____

Day 83

"Therefore encourage one another and build one another up, just as you are doing." 1 Thessalonians 5:11

One girl's voice was weary, cracked with years of pain. Another girl spoke of fear in getting married because she didn't want to lose herself. She'd had women married to Christian men say they were treated more like an older child than a competent adult with worthy thought.

Leadership should lead you to wellness, not weakness. It should lead you to cultivate your voice, not silence it. It should make you come alive, not deaden you.

Another woman who's come out of codependency says she feels alive for the first time in years, fully human, fully honest, fully *living*. She's no longer walking about, trying to be everything for her man, though she still honors, respects, and serves him. The fact that she's allowed herself to live honestly frees her right up.

The first woman is asking, "Can I speak up?" And she's asking about a matter that is backed by all of heaven because she's fighting the forces of evil. I want to cry it out, this great, big *YES!*

A man with true leadership asks for your voice. He hears your heart. He acknowledges that he's not the only one with answers, and *he's not always right.* You and your man are joint heirs with Christ, which means sometimes you hear the Lord when his way is blocked. In those cases, you must stand in truth with honor but refuse to bend for your man's approval.

When you exchange the backing of heaven over your life for the feelings of one man in your life, you exchange truth for approval, and it leaves you empty-handed, desperate, and silent. And your husband, if that's what he wants, is left lonely—because neither he nor you is honest and real at that point. He cannot be fully one with you unless he allows you to be one with God.

Jesus, I ask your forgiveness for the Christian church, who has silenced women more than cultivated them. Forgive us for giving in to cult-like tendencies in Your name.

Dare to maintain truth while maintaining your posture of honor—but never mistake giving honor for giving approval. How will you graciously love God's truth without showing disrespect to your husband?

Day 84

"The way of a fool is right in his own eyes, but a wise man listens to advice." Proverbs 12:15

Loving your husband well includes speaking into his life about needs of his heart. Many women shrink back from doing so because they are afraid of hurting their men.

One young wife asked me if she should be honest with her husband *when he asks her opinion* because she didn't want to hurt him with her honest thoughts on a need in his life. I assured her that in denying him access to her honest thoughts, she deprived him more than helped him.

Real men aren't perfect, and you are married to him for more than making him feel good about himself (though building him up is one of your goals). Sometimes, a man has destructive habits or even sins in his life, and you are the one who sees those things most clearly.

A real man receives wisdom from his wife without feeling threatened. He will know he needs her input and will show consideration for her thoughts, as he desires her to show consideration for his. Ladies, if you are stifled and cannot share with your man unless your words are affirming, there is something wrong.

Sometimes, smoothing things over is our way of keeping things smooth for ourselves.

One woman says this: "My husband is also my brother in Christ, and if I love him, I won't cover up for him, but allow God to do His work. Many wives smooth things over and fail to get out of the way when God is trying to deal with something in her man's life. I believe I also have the Spirit of Christ, and in respect and honor I refuse to smooth over things. Even though it's been hard a few times when my husband has desperately wanted my sympathy, he thanks me profusely in the end."

This woman truly honors and loves her husband, never criticizes him in public, and knows how to defer to him. They have one of the best marriages I know.

Love your man well by sharing your wellspring of wisdom!

Lord, help me speak into my husband's life and not quench Your Spirit in me. Help me share wisdom with my husband that he doesn't see. Help me do this in honor.

Dare to help your man more than alleviate conviction for your man. Do this with all honor and love, allowing God to speak clearly. What will you do when your man is feeling God's hand, and it becomes uncomfortable?

_____

_____

_____

_____

_____

_____

_____

_____

Day 85

"And all the people went up after him, playing on pipes, and rejoicing with great joy, so that the earth was split by their noise." 1 Kings 1:40

We all love being around healthy, happy people. Your man loves it, too!

Self-care is often frowned upon, and somehow wives live as if they might gain an extra diamond by running with no breath. You need not join the ranks of worn-out, downtrodden wives who stay busy but cannot stay happy.

Many wives need to slow it down and in some ways learn to live it up. Allow everyone to eat a simple breakfast so you can enjoy some quiet before the day starts. Let your husband watch the kids while you go for a walk. Whatever it takes, end the push on your heart that is taking the joy out of your life.

Your heart is a doorway; your life is not a doormat. You are not disposable, laid down for everyone to wipe their feet on anytime they choose to open the door. You are a doorway through which your man may walk to find warmth, satiation, and peace. If your doorway is falling down, he will be unable to enter.

Take time to paint your door; keep the knob updated and clean, easy for him to turn. This takes time—time to rest, repair, and nurture your heart, body, and soul.

On weekday mornings, I love taking a cup of coffee into my office for much-needed quiet while the kids eat a simple breakfast. But it took near breaking to learn that I wasn't taking *enough*. I had to realize that I wasn't loving anyone by being "needless"—I was just trying to prove myself.

Self-care could be called "marriage-maintenance." It is a gift to your husband because you will be happier, better rested, and more fun to be around—which, in the end, is the gift he truly wants. When he doesn't know how to get you there, get yourself there. Start cutting some things out so you can bring better things in.

Father, help me end this cycle of constant busyness and help me learn to breathe in the fresh air each human being needs in order to be healthy.

Today, keep giving unselfishly while you learn to receive what you need for health and vibrancy. What will you do to stay healthy for your family?

Day 86

"Now to him who is able to do far more abundantly than all that we ask or think, according to the power at work within us." Ephesians 3:20

Love your man by not taking everything personally; he is often living by his nature more than by his need.

Just as no two snowflakes are the same, no two people are the same. One may find healing in talking it out while another finds healing in processing quietly. One may be hurt by silence while the other finds solace in silence. One may feel ignored by lack of communication while the other is delaying communication to avoid more hurt.

If we can only grasp the fact that we are not the epitome of importance, that we are but a small part of a greater picture in this life, that God aims to be enjoyed and glorified in the grander sphere that our days make up, we cease to grasp quite so tightly to the small idea of perfection for the sake of our own happiness.

This is life, beautiful life.

It all ties into worship, and belief that the uniting of our spirits to the Lord is worth more than a "perfect" life. That love triumphs over the greatest transgressions, and certainly over unfulfilled expectations. That to keep love flowing in your marriage is of such great importance that you refuse to allow self-pity to rob you of love's joy.

Believe that not everything your man does (or doesn't do) is related to his love (or lack of love) for you.

Many things are simply *his nature, which we somehow attribute to his need.*

*Father, forgive me for being so self-absorbed that I relate
everything about my man right back to myself. Help me see his
nature and learn to understand it.*

Dare to enjoy the peace that comes from refusing to relate
all your man's actions to yourself. Dare to let go, and dare
to live fully, right where you are! In what areas will you
quit judging your husband today?

Day 87

"For freedom Christ has set us free; stand firm therefore, and do not submit again to a yoke of slavery." Galatians 5:1

Loving your man means you allow him to be a man, act like a man, and live like a man. Sure, you can ask him to pick up his mess or quit chewing his chips as loudly as a falling tree. But ladies who try to "domesticate" their men end up with men as depressed as tigers in cages.

We want them to stay home, help out with dishes and diapers, take us shopping, not hang out with the guys doing guy things. We want the money spent on family things instead of hunting trips, we want the career that will make the most money instead of the one that will make him happy.

We tie him tight in a noose of our own making and then wonder why he acts penned up, caged in, and moody. Sometimes we even deny him the things he needs most, like sex and respect. We become so busy asking for love that we forget to *be in love.*

Though there are times when we need and ask for his help, we make certain he is released to do his guy things. Just as you don't guilt-trip your sons for roaring trucks across the floor because your daughters may choose not to, so you don't guilt-trip your man for the things he needs simply because you don't need the same.

It's time to take a step back and look into the heart of your man. *You cannot squelch your man and keep him alive at the same time.* You cannot tie a noose about his neck, then wonder why he growls more and talks less. Love your man by releasing him to be a man!

Father, forgive me for trying to create a copy of myself so that life is better for myself. Help me never destroy who my husband was created to be.

If this section speaks to you, dare ask your husband's forgiveness, and then purpose to live differently. Learn to appreciate the wild side of him, knowing that this very characteristic is also the one that makes him want to protect you. How will you set him free from your disapproval?

Day 88

"Delight yourself in the Lord, and he will give you the desires of your heart." Psalm 37:4

It's hunting season! And it's a happy season for all of us. But it didn't used to be.

My man is hunting with our son, with his chiropractor, with his friend. And I'm loving his beard, his camouflage gear, and the smile on his face. I'm cheering them on when they're slicing through that button buck our twelve-year-old shot, and I'm sympathizing with my man over the wandering buck he tracked for a mile to no avail.

I'm also thinking back to our newlywed days when I was devastated that he wanted to play basketball rather than hang out with me. I wish I had known about my man what I know now—that he needs to play, hunt, and live aggressively because that is his nature.

Life comes in seasons, with more to learn at each turn of the road. I want us to release ourselves and our men to need different things in each season, and to be OK with those things. To accept that life will bring changes, surprises, and even hard things—*and it's all OK, and it will all be OK, as long as you follow hard after the One Who makes it all OK.*

We exist for His glory more than we live for the glory of each season. Because sometimes, seasons don't feel glorious. There have been plenty of times when I cried into my pillow with requests to God, and there have been times where I've smiled into the ceiling in utter thanks to God. Loving our men well means we accept the seasons, the lessons, the good times, and even the hard times as one more brush over God's painting on the canvas of our lives—*and we learn something with each stroke and each color of paint.*

Loving your man well includes walking each season with grace, realizing they are just that—*seasons*.

Father, thank you for bringing beauty in each season when we accept the one You have us in. Thank you for the hard seasons as well as the good seasons. Because all of them season our lives just a little more with faith and love.

Take a dare to embrace your season and learn each lesson in it. Then take a further dare and find the joy in it! How will you support your husband in his unique seasons?

Day 89

"But let your adorning be the hidden person of the heart with the imperishable beauty of a gentle and quiet spirit, which in God's sight is very precious." 1 Peter 3:4

A psychologist who studied the behavior of women once asked ladies to try a "beauty patch" for a few weeks. It was a simple, white patch worn on the arm at all times.

As days progressed, ladies reported feeling more confident, smiling at people more, and having an overall sense of greater well-being. They all returned with more care given to their hair and clothing, and brighter smiles on their faces.

The psychologist asked the ladies if they would like to know what was in the patch. She had them turn it over, only to read "nothing." The ladies' expressions turned from disbelief to gratitude as they realized they were truly beautiful and needed only to accept themselves as they were.

The psychologist called it "meaningful beauty."

To be clean, well arranged, of a healthy weight, and of pleasant appearance brings joy and satisfaction to us and those we love. But what if we do all the above, and our hearts are still not satisfied? We stare down our flaws in the mirror and exercise just a little self-hate toward the person we see.

We have forgotten that inner beauty, embracing the creation of God in ourselves, is true beauty.

Nothing is as lovely as a secure woman knowing she is a creation by a divine Creator and therefore has nothing to be discontent about. Confidence in who God created you to be (and look like) is a true gift to your man who loves you. Cultivate God-thoughts on beauty more than you covet the world's standards for beauty!

Father, help me bring the gift of confidence and peace to the atmosphere in my marriage.

Dare to refuse self-hatred and to grasp confidence! What will you speak to yourself when self-hatred puts you down?

_____

_____

_____

_____

_____

_____

_____

_____

_____

_____

_____

_____

_____

_____

_____

_____

_____

Day 90

"Where there is no guidance, a people falls, but in an abundance of counselors there is safety." Proverbs 11:14

She listened, and she listened hard. Someone older than she, wiser than she, with more experience than she was giving her wisdom in a way she'd never heard. She lifted the teacup to her lips, then grabbed a pen to jot down the life-giving words.

We're really not meant to know everything there is to know on our own. Today's dare, at the end of this book, will be for us to reach out and find mentors—older women with good marriages, wisdom, and hearts kind enough to invite us to coffee or tea.

One such woman may be at your church, or maybe you will find a blog that grabs your interest and begin writing to the author. Either way, there is no good reason for us to continue walking the death-walk toward personal and relational ruin. God has answers, and if you're not finding them on your own, allow someone to help you find them.

There is more joy to be found. There are burdens to be lifted off your weary shoulders before they become permanently stooped. There's a glorious life to be lived!

Know this—the choice is personal and one only you can make. You can live an abundant life whether or not your man gives you abundant love. In your particular situation you can find grace to thrive, whether you have a deeply rooted marriage with your best friend, or you need to leave your home because of abuse or violence.

God never leaves His daughter hanging—*ever.* He will never leave you but will lead you. Simply follow Him with a *yes* and a personal dare to get as close to His heart as you can.

Father, thank You for leading me to abundant life.
And thank You for leading me to those who will help me
discover it even faster.

Be vulnerable with those who have life to offer you. Know that you are not exempt when God hands out gifts, that your name is right on the top of the list, and He will lead you to thrive *no matter where you are,* because thriving is your gift *no matter who you are.*

You may have changed your last name, but God never changed His list of names! Who will you find, today, to help you live your tomorrows well?

_____

_____

_____

_____

_____

_____

_____

_____

_____

_____